Ple
Ce   it
Se
Pav
(206) 296-2569
www.seattleu.edu/csce

P9-DVV-222

the
promise
of
TAPPING INTO THE COLLEGE
AS A COMMUNITY ASSET
partnerships

By Jim Scheibel, Erin M. Bowley, and Steven Jones

Campus Compact

Contents

Acknowledgments

This volume was shaped in large part from the input of 40 participants at a conference on Community-Campus Partnerships held at the Wingspread Conference Center in Racine, Wisconsin, in 2003. This conference, organized by Campus Compact with support from the Ford Foundation, focused on creating a resource on community-campus partnerships for community-based organizations. Participants included directors of large and small community organizations from across the country; senior campus administrators, faculty members, and community service directors; representatives from national service and higher education associations; and national and local government representatives.[1] This book would not have been possible without the collective wisdom and experience of these Wingspread participants.

---

1. See Appendix 2 on page 95 for a list of participants.

Introduction

Nonprofit community-based organizations (CBOs) face a number of challenges in their respective communities. First is the ever-present issue of funding. Although some new sources of federal funds have become available, state and local assistance for many CBOs has been on the decline. In addition, over the past few years the combination of economic slowdown, corporate scandals, and stock market uncertainty has contributed to declines in private funding. Consequently, the environment in which many CBOs find themselves is increasingly competitive.

Second, both public and private funders demand greater accountability on the part of their grantees. Many CBOs find it necessary to expand their work to include internal program assessment in addition to fundraising and their primary mission of providing a service. This added responsibility stretches already-thin internal resources.

Third, CBOs face new challenges in terms of the issues they address and the populations they serve. For example, welfare reform has caused many CBOs to shift their focus from advocacy to training. Population changes during the 1990s, including increased immigration to the United States as well as internal population shifts, have contributed to increasing demand for adult literacy and English as a second language (ESL) programming. For example, a recent study prepared for the Nellie Mae Education Foundation found that nearly 4.3 million adults in New England need Adult Basic Education and ESL services but that fewer than 100,000 receive them.[1] These changes and others like them have left many CBOs scrambling to keep up.

---

1. Liebowitz, Marty, Amy Robins, and Jerry Rubin. *Rising to the Literacy Challenge: Building Adult Education Systems in New England.* Boston: Jobs for the Future, 2002.

The Campus as Citizen

One strategy by which CBOs can address the challenge of increasing responsibilities without a reciprocal increase in resources is to form strategic partnerships with other CBOs or with private or public-sector organizations. One potential strategic partner that is frequently over-looked by CBOs is their local institution of higher education. CBO leaders, like other community residents, often perceive colleges and universities as "ivory towers" that are in, but not of, the community.

An asset-based approach to understanding communities, however, recognizes colleges as community anchors that have enormous potential to contribute to the health and renewal of their surrounding communities. There has been a strong movement within higher education over the past 20 years to return American colleges and universities to their original mission of serving society. Campus constituencies (students, faculty, administrators, and staff), as well as external constituencies such as state legislatures, private foundations, and local community leaders, increasingly recognize the value of this role and encourage its expansion. In response, many college and university presidents are seeking to make their institutions active and responsible "citizens" in their communities.

The ways in which colleges and universities become engaged with their communities include the following activities, among others:

- Organized community-service and volunteer opportunities for students
- Faculty and student involvement in community projects through service-learning programs
- Research activities designed to address community concerns
- Sharing of resources—for example, computers, space, etc.—with CBOs
- Training and continuing education programs for nonprofit leaders and their staffs

Although such initiatives provide needed human, informational, technical, and financial resources, they are sometimes hampered in their effectiveness by a lack of input from the community. In these cases, CBOs may feel that students and faculty are using the community as a "lab"—a site for research or for placing student volunteers who may or may not have the skills, motivation, and commitment CBOs need.

Increasingly, all those involved in partnerships are recognizing that both the community and the college reap greater rewards when these activities are undertaken in the true spirit of partnership, within a reciprocal and mutually beneficial relationship. Creating this type of relationship requires establishing good communication, setting clear goals, and ensuring that the needs of all stakeholders are met. These are not simple tasks, which is where this guidebook comes in.

Campus Compact has created this book out of a desire to increase the number and improve the quality of partnerships between campuses and their communities. Campus Compact is a national coalition of more than 950 colleges and universities committed to the public purposes of higher education. Included in this mission is working to support reciprocal partnerships that contribute real benefits for the community as well as for students and their campuses.

This book describes both the wide range of partnerships that are possible and the possibilities that such partnerships open up. It offers definitions and context to help CBOs understand what colleges and universities expect from partnerships, as well as examples of what community organizations have expected and gained from partnerships. Characteristics of good partnerships, based on the experiences of CBOs that have been involved in successful partnerships, provide a foundation for those seeking to establish campus ties. On a more hands-on level, the book offers tips on how to get started and how to improve and sustain relationships.

The ultimate beneficiary of partnerships between CBOs and institutions of higher education is the community, including all those within it. Successful partnerships can help create jobs, build houses, improve the environment, boost literacy, and increase access to health care—all changes that benefit the campus as much as the rest of the community—while at the same time improving students' citizenship skills and even their academic performance. This book shows how colleges and communities can bring their assets together to make this kind of success a reality.

Using This Book

This volume specifically addresses the needs of CBOs in building partnerships with colleges and universities. While there has been a burgeoning literature in recent years on the topic of campus-community partnerships, it has been written almost entirely from the campus perspective, addressing the interests of higher education in community partnerships. This work is written from the community side of the partnership equation, addressing issues faced by community partners in working with colleges and universities.

Although this publication is organized like a book, it is not necessarily meant to be read from cover to cover. Rather, it is designed to provide you with "as-needed" information and resources to help you begin, maintain, and strengthen your partnership with your local college or university. The layout is based on the premise that partnerships between community organizations and institutions of higher education are dynamic, fluid relationships that evolve over time. Information on the following topics begins on the pages listed.

What Do You Want to Know?

What can I gain from partnering with a college or university? p. 9

How should I start planning the relationship? p. 17, 31

How do I make contact with the right people on campus? p. 25

What kinds of work can I do through a partnership? p. 37

How can I strengthen my existing partnership? p. 63, 85

How can I tell whether the benefits of my partnership outweigh the costs?
p. 78

What are some examples of successful partnerships?
p. 17, 38, 41, 46, 70, 71, 72

Where can I find more resources on campus partnerships? p. 91

The landmark work *Benchmarks for Campus/Community Partnerships* (Campus Compact, 2000) describes partnerships as developing over three stages: a beginning stage, in which partners explore common goals and values and design projects that reflect those commonalities; an intermediate stage, in which the partners build collaborative work relationships; and a final stage in which the partners work to evaluate and sustain the partnership over time. The information and resources in this book correspond with those stages. If your organization is exploring the possibility of accessing campus resources to assist with an important project, you will find practical guidelines for doing so. If your organization has already undertaken some successful projects with a higher education partner and you want to expand the partnership, you will find resources for that as well. Finally, if you want to cement your relationship, you will find examples and guidelines for building sustainability.

Part I of the book offers information on getting started, with chapters on the benefits and challenges of forming campus partnerships; the planning process; and campus organization, including how to make contact with the right people. Part II of the book outlines different types of partnership activities, with chapters on working with students, accessing resources, and establishing working relationships with faculty members. Part III looks at how to create long-term success, addressing issues that arise in sustaining partnerships and providing a framework and tools for assessing the quality and effectiveness of partnership activity.

Each section includes partnership stories that draw out the critical nuances of relationship building, as well as best practices, sample checklists, planning exercises, and other hands-on tools. Finally, the book offers a selected glossary of terms used in the world of higher education that may help CBOs in communicating with their partners, as well as a bibliography for further reading.

Although this volume is intended for use primarily by CBOs, it will undoubtedly be a valuable resource for those involved in any community-based effort on campus, including student volunteerism, community service, service-learning, and community-based research efforts. Staff members working in these areas should find this an essential tool to share with their community partners.

About the Authors

Jim Scheibel is executive director of the Community Action Partnership of Ramsey and Washington Counties (Minnesota), a nonprofit organization that makes use of campus partnerships as a vital resource in accomplishing its mission of mobilizing resources to address poverty. As a national public and nonprofit sector leader, Scheibel has gained broad experience in bringing together higher education and community groups to accomplish their goals. During the Clinton Administration, Scheibel was vice president of the Corporation for National Service, directing the AmeriCorps, VISTA, and Senior Corps programs. As an elected official, serving as a councilmember and later mayor of St. Paul, he promoted service, volunteerism, and innovative approaches to education.

Erin M. Bowley is manager of a community-based environmental education program and a nationally regarded expert on campus-based service and service-learning. She serves as an independent evaluator of service-learning and AmeriCorps programs, and provides training in community-based work-study on behalf of the national Campus Compact organization. Recently she directed the Minnesota Campus Civic Engagement Study, a project focused on documenting and measuring campus commitment to civic engagement. She served as associate director of Minnesota Campus Compact from 1994 to 2000. Bowley has an M.B.A. with an emphasis on nonprofit management, and was a Fulbright Scholar focused on comparative public policy.

Steven Jones is coordinator of the Office of Service Learning at Indiana University-Purdue University at Indianapolis (IUPUI). Formerly he was the project associate for Campus Compact's Integrating Service with Academic Studies program. He has a Ph.D. in political science from the University of Utah and was an associate professor of political science at the University of Charleston before joining Campus Compact. He compiled the second edition of the *Introduction to Service-Learning Toolkit* (Campus Compact, 2003) and is a co-author of *The Community's College: Indicators of Engagement at Two-Year Institutions* (Campus Compact, 2004). He is currently co-editing a book on teaching for civic engagement.

Part I
Getting Started

Exploring the Benefits & Challenges of Partnerships

One of the first questions that a community organization should ask when considering whether to get involved in a community-campus relationship is, "What are the benefits?" At the same time you consider the benefits, it is useful to explore what may be driving the students, faculty members, or other representatives of higher education to work with you. Knowing this information can help you be better prepared for long-term success by keeping you in touch with what motivates all parties to get involved and stay involved.

Benefits for the Community Partner

Naturally, your first concern is what the benefits of partnering are for you. Most of the benefits have to do with increased manpower, which can be allocated in any number of ways. The benefits don't end there, however. Less obvious advantages include access to knowledge, funding, facilities, and role models, among others:

- Assistance with organizational training and skill building.
- Increased pool of volunteers.
- Access to the human and physical resources of the campus.
- New funding opportunities.
- Space for community activities.
- Role models for pre-collegiate youth about the prospects of attending college.
- Assistance with program evaluation and assessment.

- Assistance with research projects.

- Assistance with advocacy and policy-related work of the organization.

- Additional expertise and resources for community development.

- Opportunity for organization staff to mentor the next generation of non-profit leaders.

See Part II of this book, beginning on page 37, for information on how to take advantage of these benefits in working with students, faculty, and others on campus.

- Opportunity to educate college faculty and staff about community issues and to work collaboratively to address those issues.

Thus, the benefits for community partners can be both specific and immediate as well as overarching and long-term. Partnering with colleges and universities can allow the CBO to enhance its capacity to achieve its mission. It can also bring the civic mission of the college in greater alignment with the local community, catalyzing multiple efforts affecting the quality of life of community residents. Partnerships focus attention on the public relevance of higher education, breaking through boundaries between the campus and the world outside the campus walls—the campus becomes part of the community and functions as an asset to the community.

The examples throughout this book highlight ways that CBOs, their clients, and their communities can reap the benefits of partnerships with local institutions of higher education. From job postings that give CBOs access to student workers to major new programs that are jointly designed and managed, partnerships offer a range of opportunities for community organizations to extend their reach and their effectiveness.

Benefits for the Campus Partner

CBOs get involved in partnerships with campuses because it helps them accomplish their social mission in concrete and practical ways. In other words, partnerships meet their organizational self-interest. The same is true for colleges and universities. Partnerships are pursued not only for the worthy ideals of community revitalization and civic renewal but also because of the practical benefits to be derived.

Institutions of higher education gain from partnerships in two ways: benefits for students and benefits for the institution as a whole.

STUDENT BENEFITS

When students are involved in community activities, a high-quality experience can offer a range of learning and other advantages:

- Real-world experience is beneficial for career exploration, skill-building, resume-building, and networking. Sometimes students even realize they need to change their career plans.

- Involvement with important concerns facing the community helps students understand the issues shaping their world, builds on their passions, and gives them skills to direct those passions in effective ways.

- Applying abstract concepts or theories to real situations helps students understand course concepts and ask valuable questions about the subjects they are learning. It can also increase their interest in the academic subject matter under study.

- Community experience can give students improved "self-efficacy"—that is, students believe that they can make a difference because they have the knowledge, skills, and self-confidence to do so.

- Students become more civically engaged; their experience can spark greater interest in social issues, politics, and understanding how to make change.

INSTITUTIONAL BENEFITS

Most institutions of higher education care first and foremost about their students. In addition to the benefits specific to students and student learning, however, community-campus partnerships offer numerous other benefits to campuses:

- Enhanced public image and stronger community or neighborhood relations help the institution's reputation in the community at large.

- A better local community (housing stock, jobs, community aesthetics) makes the institution more desirable in the eyes of prospective applicants (students, staff, and faculty) as well as alumni and donors.

- Many high school students are looking for colleges and universities that offer service and civic engagement opportunities.

- Relationships with community partners (e.g., local schools) can help the institution reach potential applicants among populations such as minority students, low-income students, and immigrants.

- Some grants require institutions to partner with a community organization to be eligible to apply.

- Faculty, administrators, and students may feel community service or community development is "the right thing to do" (from a charity, religious, or social justice perspective).

- Some institutions, programs, or groups may have community-based learning requirements that can be fulfilled only through forming partnerships with the community, such as service orientation or graduation requirements, service-learning courses, internships, or sorority/fraternity obligations.

Learning More

As you explore the possibility of partnering with your local college or university, it is important to know why the institution is interested in working with your organization. Particularly if the campus makes first contact with you (and not the other way around), you should feel comfortable asking how your organization fits into the college or university's plans. If you are not satisfied with the answers, be sure to ask follow-up questions or express your concerns. Some questions to ask include:

- Why did you choose to contact my organization?

- What motivated you to form a community partnership (or seek a community experience)?

- What do you hope to get out of this relationship (or experience, or partnership)?

- If you look back at the end of the semester (or year), what do you hope to have accomplished by partnering with my organization?

- Are there specific requirements, projects, paperwork, etc. that you need to complete during the time that we work together?

Potential Challenges

An important part of evaluating whether and how to form a campus partnership is judging the potential costs, as well as other challenges that may arise. Because community organizations and campus organizations serve different constituencies and have different operational cultures and capacities, certain issues can cause tension between CBOs and campus partners. In most cases, careful planning—including building in reciprocity, mutual respect, and open, frequent communication between the partners—can help avoid future problems.

See pp. 79–82 for tools to evaluate the costs and benefits of a partnership.

FINANCIAL COSTS

Financial costs to the organization may include the following:

- Time and materials needed to train, supervise, and evaluate students or participate in research.

- Time spent in planning and coordinating partnership activities.

- Material costs—for example, space and resources dedicated to partnership activities.

Although in most cases the financial gain outweighs the financial costs of partnerships for the CBO, it is important to anticipate costs as part of the planning process.

THE ACADEMIC CALENDAR

The academic calendar is quite different from the standard 12-month calendar. In general, college students and faculty members will be available only 8 months out of the year, with several breaks within that 8-month period. The 8 months will generally be divided into two 15–16 week semesters or three 10-week quarters or trimesters. Colleges on a semester system generally run from late August to mid-May, with a 3- to 4-week break for the winter holidays and at least one additional break in the spring. Colleges on a quarter system usually start classes in mid- to late September and end in late May or early June.

Students who are working with your organization may be available only for a single semester or quarter period. Because students plan their time around the academic calendar, including exam periods, they can appear to be flighty and unreliable from the CBO's perspective. Faculty members also plan their work around the academic calendar, with the summer months being particularly sacrosanct for scholarly work.

Although it may be challenging to work around the academic calendar, it is not impossible. The key to getting the most out or your collaboration with colleges while working with their schedule is to know the calendar and plan ahead. You can find a copy of your local college's academic calendar on their website and in their yearly college catalog.

See p. 34 for tips on working around the academic calendar.

POWER DIFFERENTIALS

In almost all cases, the campus partner will have more resources than the community partner. This does not necessarily mean that the campus partner has more power, especially if power is defined in terms of influence and credibility among community residents. Still, the unequal position between community and campus partners in terms of resources and personnel can be a real source of conflict, especially when the question arises as to who controls the process of allocating resources to the partnership. It is important to lay out in advance how resource determinations will be made and by whom, as well as what each partner's obligations will be.

DIFFERENT VALUES AND PRIORITIES

Most community organizations have a specific mission with matching priorities, whereas the campus partner has multiple missions and priorities. In most cases, one or more of those multiple campus missions and priorities will overlap with yours. However, the degree of attention paid to those overlapping priorities may differ between the community and campus partners. Furthermore, the students and faculty with whom you work may or may not share your organization's values and commitments.

Ideally, students and faculty who may be personally uncomfortable with the work of a particular agency would not work with that agency to begin with, but that is not always the case. It is essential to make sure that potential campus partners understand your mission, goals, and expectations, as well as factors such as site location and populations served, before setting up a partnership.

LANGUAGE

Both community organizations and institutions of higher education have specialized language. In addition, each academic discipline has its own jargon that may be confusing to people outside of that field of study. Lack of understanding of each other's specialized language can lead to misunderstandings and marginalization of one partner or of a partner's staff and/or constituents.

Again, careful planning is they key. If you have a website, an annual report, or other documentation that explains your work using your terminology, make sure to share them with campus personnel. You should do the same, reviewing the campus website and other available materials and asking questions up front. Avoid jargon where possible; where it cannot be avoided, make sure that the terminology used by both parties is explicitly defined in any partnership conversations or documents to avoid misunderstandings.

See Appendix 3, p. 99, for a glossary of higher education terminology.

FACULTY INCENTIVES

As with most professions, faculty members are evaluated on certain elements of job performance. The three traditional areas of faculty evaluation are teaching, research (or "scholarship"), and service. (Service is traditionally defined as service to the institution or academic department; it rarely refers to service in the community outside the campus.) At most institutions, it is difficult for faculty to show that community work is relevant to their evaluation. This is the result of a system that values classroom teaching and scholarship that is objective, formal, and published in academic journals.

This system is one of the greatest barriers to advancing campus-community partnerships, especially where faculty are involved. Even at institutions where the official guidelines for faculty promotion and tenure do not exclude community work, the culture related to the process may discourage it. At a small number of institutions this is changing, and the guidelines for faculty promotion and tenure are being rewritten or reinterpreted to include high-quality community work. In addition, among community colleges, as well as some public universities (e.g., with faculty unions) and other schools, traditional evaluation measures are not as rigid or important.

It may be worth asking faculty members about the evaluation system they are involved in at their college or university. How do community-based teaching and scholarship fit within their evaluation criteria? Understanding the complex pressures involved in faculty evaluation, promotion, and tenure can give CBOs insight into the basis for the actions and decisions of faculty members.

The Planning Process

Before any type of partnership activity begins, it is important to establish a planning process to manage key elements of the partnership, including communication, funding, and marketing/public relations. Even aspects of the partnership that won't arise until later on, such as evaluation and celebration of work completed, should be included in the initial planning.

Planning for Success: The Family Investment Center

The Family Investment Center, which provides adult basic education and general equivalency degree (GED) testing, has a partnership with Hibbing Community and Technical College in Hibbing, MN, in which college students provide tutoring and other services. The relationship with the college started when several faculty members who were interested in starting a service-learning initiative (in which students work in the community to gain relevant experience in their academic field while providing a needed service) called the center's director, Renee Tomatz. Tomatz worked with the faculty members to identify other community partners and create a service-learning program.

A BROADER ROLE

In addition to working with students in her child care and adult literacy programs, Tomatz has been invited to sit on college advisory boards to provide input on recruiting and retaining students for the school's nursing program as well as on developing programs such as computer literacy for nontraditional students. Her advice and expertise have helped the college effectively recruit

(continued...)

new students from the low-income population she serves and to identify potential barriers to their success. Tomatz also refers interested candidates to Hibbing and makes person-to-person contacts so that prospective students will find a friendly face at the college.

When Tomatz received a fellowship from the Blandin Foundation to work on diversity issues in the community, she designed a community-based mentoring system for students of color at Hibbing. She recruited families in the area to mentor the students by having them over for meals, including them in activities, and providing guidance. This program has helped the community become more accepting of students of color while educating students about the community and improving retention among these students.

MUTUAL BENEFITS

The partnership works because everyone benefits. Tomatz gets the extra bodies she needs for programs for which she can't afford to hire staff. Her clients enjoy working with the college students, and the students gain new insight into their fields of study. The students also learn about new career opportunities—some have even changed career plans.

The college has also benefited from the partnership. In addition to improved admission and retention of student populations, the college has gained a better reputation in the community. Whereas many community members once saw the college as isolated, the community now sees the college as a resource. Community organizations make greater use of the college's space and resources, having realized that those resources are not there just for the students.

PLANNING AND RELATIONSHIPS

In giving advice to others, Tomatz stresses the need for careful planning. It is important to design the program to meet the needs of both sides, so that everyone can benefit. In particular, CBOs need to think about students' academic needs and to be aware that different classes may have different requirements. One key aspect of planning is to design experiences that will make students really want to come.

Tomatz also notes the importance of planning around the campus calendar. Holidays and exam periods can cause coordination challenges, but up-front

(continued...)

planning can help smooth scheduling. One aspect of scheduling that may not be obvious is the need to plan time for "closure" when students complete their work at your site. Closure is important for vulnerable populations; CBOs should know when students' last day will be and prepare clients for the students' departure.

According to Tomatz, having a lot of communication and dialogue before getting the partnership up and running results in a stronger program. Committing the time up front to know each other pays off in the long term. Finally, she notes the need to recognize that you're not just building a program; you need to build a *relationship,* so you can head off problems and deal with any issues that arise.

Communication

Communication is the single most important aspect of planning an effective partnership. Effective communication can smooth the relationship by clarifying expectations, helping to establish concrete goals, heading off problems, and establishing a culture of mutual respect. Following are steps for establishing communication channels and protocols that will form the foundation of the partnership.

Identify one primary contact person. Communication is easier and clearer when you identify one person on campus to communicate with most of the time. This person can also act as a guide to other resources at the institution. If you are the one initiating contact, don't be discouraged if the first person you talk with can't help—keep searching for the best contact.

"Campus Organization and Contact Points," beginning on p. 25, offers information on where and how to make initial contact.

Determine whether you need to contact faculty members. If you are working with students who are receiving academic credit for their community work, you may need to initiate communication through their instructor. It is not unreasonable to expect the instructor to visit your organization and meet with you to clarify expectations.

Decide how you will communicate. Once the initial contact is made, whether by the campus or the CBO, it is essential to have a plan for continued communication. Make sure to find out the best way to contact people and set procedures and timetables for maintaining communication. Try to establish communication procedures that take into account all parties' preferences and schedules. This may mean mixing less formal communication such as email or telephoning with in-person meetings (see below).

Strive to meet face-to-face. No matter how busy everyone is, try to arrange at least one early meeting in person with your primary campus contact person and others with whom you interact. Building a personal relationship will enhance other forms of communication later. Invite campus people to meet at your office, and offer to meet on campus, too. Email can be very effective for staying in touch at other times; students, instructors, and others in higher education can be difficult to find at their desk but tend to use email regularly.

Learn the language and culture of higher education. Don't hesitate to ask your higher education partner about acronyms and higher education terminology. Offer to clarify your organization's and community's culture and terminology for students, instructors, and staff from the campus.

Put yourself on an equal footing. Don't be intimidated by academic degrees or complex higher education systems. Some academics may be awed by your first-hand experience and successes. Be persistent in finding people at higher education institutions who are respectful and excited to work with you.

Write down goals and expectations. Even if you have a very informal relationship, you can benefit from taking the time to clarify and write down the expectations and goals of all parties involved. One way to ensure that this happens is to offer to record expectations and share them with your higher education partners for feedback. If your partner already has a standard contract or "learning agreement," make sure that *your* goals and expectations are also recorded, either by adding them or by creating an additional document if needed.

Funding

Although many forms of partnership do not require outside funding, others—particularly more involved partnerships that involve establishing structures and programs—may require financial backing to ensure sustainability. In these cases, planning a fundraising strategy up front is important for success.

Collaborate on fundraising for best results. Like nonprofits, many campuses are strapped for funds. Don't expect to receive cash from your partner, but don't hesitate to explore the possibilities. Plan a fundraising strategy together. A campus might help you receive funds from an unlikely source, or vice versa. Foundations and corporations like funding good partnerships, and some fund *only* collaborative efforts, so present a united voice in your meetings and proposals.

Put relationships first, grant writing second. Very few grant proposals are funded without some human contact prior to submitting the proposal. Think about who at the campus or in the community might have personal contacts to use. Attempt to meet with foundation staff, program officers, or individual donors to find out whether your work is a good match for their interests. Follow up on any positive signals from the meeting with a strong written proposal.

Don't forget in-kind contributions. Keep in mind that colleges and universities offer the possibility of many types of in-kind contributions. Examples include meeting rooms, public relations staff, and technical expertise.

Marketing/PR

Publicizing the work of your partnership can have a range of benefits: It can increase participation in your project, raise awareness among funders, and motivate the partners to remain involved. A campus-community partnership may offer different opportunities for publicity than a CBO or campus could expect on its own. Collaboration to take advantage of these opportunities can benefit all involved.

Tap into new publicity avenues. Higher education institutions in general like to show that they have positive connections in their local community. Many campuses have sophisticated offices dedicated to PR and publicity that can help write press releases or generate media attention. A good project might be publicized in the college newsletter, e-newsletters, and other publications, helping you reach new audiences.

Jointly plan a marketing strategy. Make sure to be at the table when discussing how to showcase your project or partnership for others. The time it takes to plan for effective marketing of your project will pay off in increased visibility and awareness, including awareness among corporate and other donors who might be excited by your project.

Evaluation

Evaluation is as important as other aspects of planning. By agreeing in advance on what you want to know about the project or partnership (what you will assess), you gain a stronger voice in how the partnership is put together. You'll also have more chance of gathering needed information on how the partnership is working if you build evaluation in at the beginning rather than waiting until everyone is busy with the project itself.

Jointly plan the evaluation. Discuss and agree on what you want to know about the project up front. You may find out that you and your higher education partner are interested in very different things. How will you know if your partnership or work together has been successful? Determine what kinds of measurement strategies will be effective, keeping in mind the education goals of the campus as well as the community issue you address and the people who might be involved. Create a written plan that includes your goals or objectives, how they will be measured, and how the results will be used.

Get information from all involved. Involving all parties in the evaluation process can help you get the best information on how well your work together is going. This is important for knowing what strengths you can build on and what needs to be improved. An inclusive process also validates and respects all parties' opinions and may help you avoid problems down the road.

Ask your partner for assistance. Campuses usually have faculty and other resources that can help with tools for measuring results. Be sure that any ready-made assessment tool either meets your specific needs or can be adapted to do so.

See "Assessing Partnerships," beginning on p. 75, for additional information on evaluating partnerships.

Celebrating

It's important to make time to acknowledge the contributions of the project's partners and participants. One way to do this is to create opportunities to bring all participants together—members of the community, your organization, and campus representatives—to meet each other and share their perceptions of the project. Let people express what makes them proud to be part of the project, and what they hope for the future of the partnership.

Celebrate the small. Celebration doesn't always mean big events. You don't have to wait until the end of a project or year—celebrate benchmarks along the way. Small, inexpensive tokens of appreciation throughout a project, such as handwritten cards, special food at meetings, or learning and remembering birthdays, can make a difference in morale and motivation.

Be inclusive and creative. Many projects involve people of diverse cultural backgrounds. This is an opportunity to celebrate in different ways. If you are planning an event, including food, music, or other cultural traditions can enliven the occasion and make it more meaningful. Don't forget to include board members, trustees, college officials, and other civic leaders. It may help them participate if you offer them a special role in the celebration, such as welcomer or host.

Trade places. It's good to bring campus partners to the community and community members and participants to campus. If you usually spend time one place or the other, consider changing locations at least once. It will give all involved a different perspective that may be useful in future work.

Campus Organization & Contact Points

In considering any type of partnership activity, the first thing to do is learn about your local or regional institutions of higher education. Before beginning this process, it is useful to know what types of institutions exist and how their differences may affect how—and even whether—they approach community partnerships. This information can help you choose which college or university to approach and how best to make your case.

This chapter outlines some of the different kinds of institutions you may encounter, as well as how campuses are structured to work with the community and where you can go find the right people to start a conversation about a possible partnership.

Types of Higher Education Institutions

Higher education institutions may be two- or four-year, public or private, research-oriented, faith-based, or focused on any of a number of other areas. Knowing the structure and priorities of your local institution can help you in planning your initial contact as well as any subsequent partnership activity. The major breakdowns of institutional types follow.

TWO-YEAR INSTITUTIONS

Community colleges and technical colleges (sometimes known as junior colleges or vocational schools) award two-year associate degrees or certificates rather than four-year bachelor's degrees. They generally serve local populations; they may prepare students for work or to transfer to a four-year institution.

Partnering with community colleges offers several advantages. First, because community college students usually live locally, many are already familiar with the community you serve and with the issues your agency addresses. Some of these students are actively looking to "give back" to their communities, applying the knowledge and skills they are acquiring in college. Second, community college faculty are committed to teaching (as opposed to research), and are likely to see the educational benefits of having students learn through work at your agency. Third, community colleges have an institutional mission to serve the communities in which they are located. They want to be known as the "community's college" and see themselves as public spaces and economic engines for community development. Finally, community colleges frequently have partnerships with local government and businesses that you may be able to tap into.

On the other hand, there are some limitations to partnering with community colleges. For example, community college faculty have heavy teaching loads and consequently do not have a lot of spare time for doing community research or designing community-based learning experiences for their students. Similarly, a high percentage of community college students attend class full-time while working 20-30 hours a week and/or taking care of families. These students may not have time for becoming involved at community agencies.

FOUR-YEAR INSTITUTIONS
Four-year colleges and universities award bachelor's degrees after the equivalent of four years of study. The distinction between a college and a university is that colleges may offer only bachelor's degrees, while universities offer master's degrees and usually doctoral degrees (for example, Ph.D. or M.D.).

Universities offer some partnership benefits that two- and even four-year colleges cannot. Because of their size and research orientation, universities have a wider variety of academic and research programs than most colleges. In addition, the university may have a law school and/or medical school that can provide assistance to community legal and medical clinics. On the other hand, a college may devote more attention to its teaching responsibilities and is a potential source for committed students and faculty who can help with community organizing and advocacy work.

PUBLIC OR PRIVATE

Colleges and universities can be either public or private. Public colleges and universities are state-supported and receive a significant share of their funding from state legislatures. Private colleges and universities rely primarily on student tuition, private gifts, and grant funding.

Knowing the distinction between private and public schools can help in planning the initial stages of your partnership. For example, most state colleges and universities have a public mandate to apply their teaching and research activities to meeting public needs. Many private colleges, especially faith-based colleges, have historical missions based in service and social justice. Identifying the specific public mandate or private mission of local campuses will help you understand their motivations as well as assist you in crafting a compelling argument as you seek their support.

Making Contact

One of the greatest difficulties in beginning a community-campus partnership is figuring out where to start. From the outside, with their brick and cement walls, campuses can seem uninviting and a bit intimidating. In addition, trying to identify somebody to talk to on campus can be a challenge, given that the campus listings in the phone book may take up a page or more. Few campuses have an office labeled "community partnerships." How should you contact the campus? Who is the right person to discuss possible partnership opportunities, and how can you find that person?

You may want to start by considering whether you know anyone who works at or attends the local college or university. This person may be able to help interpret how the institution is organized to work with the community and may be able to tell you exactly who to talk with, make an introduction, or at least give you ideas about where to start. You can find a guide by considering your own or your organization's current connections to the campus. You may save yourself multiple phone calls and dead ends by taking full advantage of your networks first.

If you do not have any such connections, look for one of the following campus departments or offices. Start with a campus directory or go to the college or university website for department listings.

COMMUNITY SERVICE OFFICE

Campus Compact's 2004 annual member survey found that 86% of member campuses have a community service or service-learning office to coordinate campus service programs. Most of these centers have a full- or part-time director dedicated to these efforts, and some have full staffs. If your local campus has such an office, this is the place to start. Check under these names:

- Volunteer Center or Office
- Community Service Office
- Service-Learning Office
- Community Connections
- Community Partnerships
- Campus-Community Partnerships
- America Reads (for tutoring/literacy programs)
- Tutoring (or Mentoring) program
- Other offices with the word "service" or "community" in the title

OTHER CAMPUS OFFICES

If, after your initial search, you still haven't been able to establish a contact on campus, what is your next step? Even when the campus doesn't have a single office or department in charge of campus-community partnerships, many other offices may organize volunteers or support work in the community. If you are struggling to connect with one office or person on campus, the following may be useful places to try.

Public Relations or Neighborhood Relations. Virtually all institutions have some sort of public relations (PR) office. If the campus has a centralized office that coordinates community partnerships or service, the public relations office should be able to help locate it.

Internships or Career Center. Most institutions list internships (both paid and unpaid) through their academic departments, and in some cases through one central office that may be called the Internships Office, Career Center, or a similar title.

Student Clubs. Student organizations such as political organizations (Campus Democrats, Republicans, Greens); departmental groups such as the Sociology or Education Club; sororities and fraternities; academic honors clubs; special interest groups such as PIRGs or Habitat for Humanity; and many others may choose to do projects in the community. A list of the heads of these organizations can usually be found through a campus office such as Campus Programs, Campus Activities, Student Activities, Student Leadership, or something similar.

Residential Life. Residential Life is usually the name of the office that organizes the activities of on-campus student housing (dorm life). At many institutions, the student coordinator of each floor (the resident assistant, or RA) may be responsible for coordinating community projects. At some institutions, entire floors (or townhouses or other units of campus housing) take on the theme of working in the community.

Campus Ministry. Student groups and campus offices intended to help explore and develop faith in various religions may also have a focus or program for work in the community.

Athletics. At many institutions, student athletes are involved as mentors and volunteer coaches in the community.

Work-Study or Financial Aid Office. At present, all institutions are required to spend at least 7% of the resources they receive in Federal Work-Study funds on community-based placements. By locating the person on campus who coordinates student employment or work-study (usually in the Student Financial Aid office), community organizations can inquire how to become a community work-study host.

See pp. 42–43 for more information on how Federal Work Study programs work.

Academic Departments. Many individual departments organize their own relationships with the community. Typical academic departments that have connections in the community include Education, Sociology, Political Science, and Urban Studies. In addition, many professional programs, such as Nursing, Social Work, Law, and Medicine require or strongly encourage work in the community.

Dean or Vice-Presidents' Offices. In rare cases, community programs are organized through the office of the Dean of Students or the Vice President for Student (or Academic) Affairs. Although most of these offices do not directly organize campus-community programs, they should be aware of other offices that do.

Extension Office. Some institutions, often in rural settings, have an "extension" office based in each county. Another growing trend is Internet-based partnerships across long distances. Try the extension office for information on such programs.

CAMPUS COMPACT OFFICES

Campus Compact has contact information for personnel responsible for campus-community partnerships at each of its 950+ member colleges and universities. Campus Compact has 30 state offices across the country, as well as a national office and five regional consortia, that provide training, resources, networks, and forums to help campuses and communities connect. To find an office in your area, go the national Campus Compact website at www.compact.org/membership.

Partnership Planning Resources

Questions to Ask Before Starting a Partnership

1 What will the costs of the partnership be to your organization?

2 What value will partnering add? Does your potential partner have resources that would be useful to your organization? Does the opportunity to help educate college students appeal to you and your staff?

3 What necessary preparation will you need to make? Are your organizational priorities clearly articulated? Can you effectively communicate them to your partner?

4 Do your organization's needs and your potential partner's assets complement each other? What about their needs and your assets? What role do you or your staff play in the design of partnership activities?

5 Have you carefully examined potential conflicts between you and your partner? Can your organization work with or around the academic calendar? Can your potential partner accept the constraints created by your organization's clients and other obligations?

Source: Royer, K. *Strengthening Collaboration Between Higher Education and Communities.* Indianapolis: Indiana Campus Compact, 2000, p. 12 (www.iupui.edu/~icc/publications.htm). Reprinted by permission.

10 Steps for Developing a Partnership

1 Create a vision for where you want the partnership to be in one year, two years, and more.

2 Create a mission statement by taking the mission statements of each organization into consideration.

3 Map out the resources and capacities of individuals, organizations, and local campuses.

4 Build community relationships based on local assets for mutually beneficial problem-solving within the community.

5 Mobilize the communities' assets fully for developing the partnership and sharing information.

6 Convene as broadly representative a group as possible for the purposes of building a community vision and plan.

7 Create goals, objectives, and an action plan with a timeline to support the mission.

8 Develop a means to evaluate and monitor the progress of the partnership.

9 Leverage activities, investments, and resources from outside the community to support the development of the partnership.

10 Develop a plan to communicate with others about the partnership, publicize the partnership's efforts, and celebrate and recognize its accomplishments.

Planning Exercise:
Matching Expertise with Project Needs and Goals

1 What is the nature of the activity under consideration?

2 What are the anticipated results of the activity?

3 What technical expertise is required of the campus? (For example, professional knowledge and skills—health care, legal, business, etc.—computer expertise, research design and analysis.)

4 What level of technical expertise is required of the campus? Is the degree of
   technical expertise required for the activity relatively high or relatively low?

5 What level of community involvement/participation is necessary? For example, will the activity require convening citizens' groups or mobilizing individuals to attend a health fair or similar event? Are community members (students
   at a school, residents of a nursing home, clients at a shelter) already in place?

6 What are the risks to each partner should the results of the activity not meet
   expectations? For example, would faculty members lose academic prestige?
   Would CBOs lose clients' trust or funding from private and/or public funders?

7 Who will be involved in the activity? Does the activity involve collaboration
   among several CBOs and campus constituents, or does it involve a small
   number of individuals from a single CBO and one academic department?

8 What specific resources/assets are necessary to achieve the desired results—
   e.g., financial, technical, or organizational resources?

9 Does the activity align with the traditional functions of the partners? For
   example, does it fit with the traditional teaching and research mission of the
   college or university? Does it fit with the outreach/service mission of the
   CBO?

10 Does the activity require the appointment of a leader—that is, a point person
   who will coordinate the individuals and activities? Does that person have
   credibility and support among both community and campus constituencies?

Tips for Working around the Academic Calendar

1 If you will be working with faculty members, make your initial contact with them at least two or three weeks before the academic period begins. If you are planning on working with a particular faculty member in the fall, you may need to initiate contact before the spring session has ended.

2 If you need student volunteers, contact the college or university at the beginning of the academic term. By the third week or so of the term, most institutions have completed their volunteer coordination for that period.

3 Be prepared for requests from the college to host community service events during Freshman Orientation week (usually the third or fourth week of August) and around certain holidays, such as Martin Luther King Day.

4 Find out from faculty and students when in-term exams and holidays are and plan not to have students at your sites during those times.

5 In particular, don't be overly reliant on student volunteers if you need extra staffing during the November-December holiday period. Students frequently travel during that period and usually also have their final exams then.

Part II
Partnership Activities

Working with College Students

Relationships between higher education institutions and community organizations can be as simple as hosting a volunteer or intern, or as complex as launching a community economic development initiative that involves hundreds of people sharing resources and expertise. Traditionally, many campus-community relationships have been characterized as *placements*, where students or others are placed in an organization to complete a task. Increasingly, there is recognition that these relationships might be more effective as *partnerships*, where the needs and resources of both higher education and communities are defined and decisions are made jointly. If your organization has never worked with a higher education institution, placement activities may be exactly what you need. However, as your relationship with the students, faculty, and staff of the campus grows, you will probably want to move beyond placement to partnership.

This chapter focuses on partnership activities that involve students. Student work in the community takes two forms: curricular activity, which is completed as part of a course, and co-curricular activity, which is not part of a course. Because curricular activity has an academic component, part of the community organization's responsibility is to work with students to ensure that their community experiences help them understand their coursework. Co-curricular activity, which encompasses more traditional volunteer work, does not have the same academic focus, but it is still useful to encourage students to think about the larger impact of the organization and their work within it.

"Something Beautiful": The Pike Market Senior Center

The Pike Market Senior Center in Seattle has partnered with both the University of Washington and Seattle Central Community College since 1992. These partnerships have involved hundreds of students from a variety of disciplines. To recruit students, the center sends job descriptions to the University of Washington's Carlson Center, which has a small, centralized staff. The Carlson Center educates campus faculty and staff about teaching and research opportunities with nonprofit organizations.

Students have worked with their faculty, the Senior Center's staff, and seniors served by the center to develop a number of educational and recreational activities. Following are just a few examples:

- Anthropology students created a panel to discuss different cultural traditions related to death and dying.

- Students in a course on world hunger and resource development researched services for providing food and other resources to low-income people. Based on their findings, students conducted a forum on hunger with seniors and identified local programs and services.

- Students who were studying the coffee trade held a coffee tasting event that included presentations on the geography and economics of coffee around the world.

- Students in various disciplines developed dialogues on health care, housing, personal relationships, and other topics.

- Art and communication students produced a talent show conducted for and by seniors, complete with publicity.

Nola Freeman, director of the Pike Market Senior Center, understands that such experiences are beneficial both for the students and for the agency's clients. "Something beautiful is happening here," she says. "Seniors participate in the [students'] learning. By sharing their life experiences, they contribute to the [students'] body of knowledge. Because seniors have something to offer and their experience counts, their self-esteem is raised."

Curricular Activity

Students are often able to count work in or with the community toward the completion of their college degree. These experiences can fulfill

either general graduation requirements or specific academic requirements, in which case they generate "credit hours" toward a course.

SERVICE-LEARNING

Service-learning has been one of the largest areas of growth in partnerships between higher education and community organizations in recent
years, gaining strong momentum at many campuses in the 1990s and
into the 2000s. Service-learning is a process in which an academic course
includes student participation in meaningful community work that rein-
forces course concepts. Service-learning has been shown to contribute to
students' academic understanding, civic development, personal or career
growth, and understanding of larger social issues.

For example, students in a basic chemistry course may take samples of
paint from a low-income housing development to learn to test for lead,
as opposed to testing traditional samples prepared in a lab. In addition to
learning a basic lab skill, students also learn about larger social issues
related to housing and poverty—applications of chemistry in the "real
world." In return, the nonprofit housing developer receives data it can
use to improve the safety of people's homes.

Students are typically required to complete 1 to 3 hours of community
work per week over a 10- to 15-week term or semester, although there is
great variation in what might be required. In some courses, service-
learning experiences are an option for additional credit or can replace a
more traditional assignment, while in other courses the entire class is
required to participate. Since the term *service-learning* describes both a
way of teaching and learning and an experience, it can be considered a
larger umbrella under which other experiences, such as community-
based research or some internships, may fall.

It is important to know that that there is debate regarding whether
nonacademic experiences should be described as service-learning, and
that the answer may vary from one campus to the next. This debate can
affect your work in several ways. If the label *service-learning* is used to
describe volunteer work without any academic requirement, you may
have difficulty enlisting faculty support. Faculty members are more likely
to participate in community work if they believe that it is tied to their

students' academic content and learning. On the other hand, when service-learning is tied to academic work, faculty members may (and in fact should) ask you to participate in the course or to help design the course syllabus. This participation is beneficial, as it gives your organization a greater say in how the work will be performed, but it requires some extra work.

COMMUNITY-BASED RESEARCH

Community-based research, also called action research or participatory action research, has also grown in recent years. Students and faculty conduct community-based research in order to address community-identified issues. Instead of relying solely on the library or the Internet for information, students can meet with community residents to understand the issues and problems guiding their research.

Ideally, the research is planned in collaboration with community representatives and the results are shared with the community. In one project, for example, students and faculty from a landscape architecture class at the University of Michigan were working on a design project to transform an old, unused city park into a child-friendly space. As part of the planning process, the college students toured the area with local first and second graders to get their vision of how the park should look.[1]

INTERNSHIPS

Students may complete an internship that is paid or unpaid, working independently or as part of a group seminar. Internships generally engage students in "real-life" work experiences meant to contribute to the students' understanding of a career field and/or help them develop useful skills and knowledge. Student interns usually work 10–40 hours a week for an organization. They receive supervision from a faculty member as well as from organization staff and usually have a learning plan or goals for the internship. Some institutions offer group internships, where students meet as a class during their internship.

---

1. A full account of this project is described by David Scobey, director of the Arts of Citizenship Program at the University of Michigan, in "Putting the Academy in Its Place: A Story about Park Design, Civic Engagement, and the Research University." Available online at www.artsofcitizenship.umich.edu/about/02102000.html.

THE PRACTICUM

A practicum is similar to an internship in that it gives the student extended, on-site experience. However, a practicum is more specifically geared toward providing a real-world work experience that involves the direct application of skills learned in the classroom. Common examples of this type of work include student teaching and clinical experience in health care fields such as nursing or chiropractic. Some business disciplines, such as accounting, may also require students to fulfill a practicum. Students participating in a practicum do their work under the supervision of an experienced on-site practitioner.

Students as Partners: The Cooperative Feeding Program

The Cooperative Feeding Program (CFP), an emergency service provider to homeless families and individuals in Ft. Lauderdale, Florida, has partnerships with three local universities—Nova Southeastern University, Barry University, and Florida International University. "Invaluable" is the way Lisa Margulis, director of social services at CFP, describes these partnerships.

When Margulis first began working with students, they basically provided extra hands, serving food and stocking the pantry. As the program progressed, students moved into the dining room and practiced case management. The more the students got involved, the more valuable their knowledge became. Margulis began to integrate students' insights and experiences into program management, thus strengthening her group's services. Eventually she and the staff started seeing the students as partners rather than just "volunteers," and engaged them in program planning and evaluation.

The benefits are two-way. The CFP partnership gives the students opportunities to become involved in the community and to develop and use practical skills before graduation. In addition, students learn first-hand the strengths and needs of different communities.

Margulis believes that the more the students help design the project, the more ownership they feel. The result is that students are more motivated and reliable, and they are able to provide a higher quality of service to CFP and its clients.

Co-Curricular Activity

VOLUNTEERISM

Volunteers from higher education may find their way to community organizations through many avenues. College or university volunteer experiences may be either one-time or ongoing, with the first often leading to the second:

- **One-time or short-term service.** Individuals or groups may look for one-time or very short-term volunteer experiences for a variety of reasons: to fulfill a requirement (such as a "day of service" for new student orientation), to share a common experience (for example, among all the students in a club or on an athletic team), or simply because they are motivated to "give back" or get involved without making a long-term commitment. One common example is the "alternative break," where students do service projects during school vacations.

- **Ongoing volunteer commitments.** Individual students, student groups, or the institution may organize individuals or groups to make a commitment to volunteer each week or month at a particular organization.

Volunteer activities may be sponsored and actively encouraged by the institution, or they may reflect individual students' interests and commitment. Some institutions try to establish ongoing relationships with a certain key community partner organizations, including K-12 schools, food pantries, and others. In those cases, the commitment might be made by the institution to send volunteers regularly to a certain organization. In other cases, individuals from an institution simply respond to a notice for volunteers or search for their own opportunities.

COMMUNITY SERVICE FEDERAL WORK-STUDY

All institutions of higher education that receive funding from the federal government as part of the Federal Work-Study (FWS) program are required to spend at least 7% of those funds on community-based work-study placements. In other words, while work-study students typically work 5–20 hours on campus in positions such as food service worker, department secretary, or library assistant, some students at each institution must complete their work-study position in a community-serving setting.

Although many campuses have strong community FWS programs and are well above the minimum required 7% community work figure, campuses often struggle to coordinate these efforts. Many institutions are looking to work with community organizations to help host students in community FWS positions. This can be a good way to start a relationship with a college or university, since it is helping the institution meet a federal requirement.

In community FWS programs, the community organization usually pays a portion of students' wages. The amount can range from as little as 0% to as much as 50%, but typically the community organization pays between 10% and 30%. One common program, America Reads, is often an exception. Students working in America Reads programs help tutor children or serve in family literacy programs. In many of these cases, the college or university pays 100% of the students' wages through its FWS funds.

Work-study experiences in the community usually do not involve course credit, but there are some exceptions. Programs such as America Reads may offer a course that supplements the work-study experience. In these cases, students are taking a course on a subject matter (e.g., child and adult literacy issues) while also completing relevant work-study hours in the community.

To find out how to host a work-study student at your organization, contact the Financial Aid or Student Employment office at your local college or university.

AMERICORPS AND VISTA

Some campuses participate in AmeriCorps, a federal service program that encourages people to serve their community in a full- or part-time capacity in exchange for a modest living allowance and education scholarship. AmeriCorps students typically commit 10–20 hours per week in the community in direct service roles (tutoring children, building low-income housing, etc.).

Some campuses host VISTA volunteers, who officially are also AmeriCorps members. VISTA volunteers work full-time coordinating programs that serve low-income people. VISTAs do not serve directly, but instead coordinate others who serve. Your primary liaison on campus with respect to coordinating service-learning and student volunteer activities may well be a VISTA volunteer. AmeriCorps and VISTA are coordinated by a federal agency called the Corporation for National and Community Service (CNCS).

LEARN & SERVE AMERICA

Federal funds from CNCS support college and K-12 service-learning experiences through the Learn and Serve America program. Colleges may have access to these funds for faculty and student initiatives through state Campus Compact offices.

Campus Resources and Working with Faculty

Volunteers and interns are important community assets, but higher education can offer many additional resources. While many partnerships begin through a single personal connection, usually involving student work, it is valuable for community organizations to be aware of the multiple types of resources and programs that higher education might offer in addition to activities that involve students. This chapter outlines the range of possibilities that exist when campuses and communities work together.

Community engagement activities that may not involve students include:

- Facility sharing,
- Sharing of individual expertise,
- Faculty research,
- Sharing of academic resources, and
- Community development initiatives.

Facility Sharing

Most colleges and universities have tremendous physical resources, such as classrooms and other meeting spaces, computer labs, theaters, art galleries, athletic facilities, green spaces, residence halls, libraries, and more. Some campuses make these facilities available to the public on a free or low-cost basis, while others have more restricted access. Of those that charge for facilities use, some have a nonprofit or community partner rate. Some campuses have worked with community or government

From Enemies to Allies: GRASS Routes

GRASS Routes (Grass Roots Activism, Sciences, and Scholarship), a project that unites the work of campus researchers and community members, came together through the work of three partners: Susan Gust, neighborhood activist and member of the Phillips neighborhood Healthy Housing Collaborative; Cathy Jordan, assistant professor of pediatrics and neurology, University of Minnesota; and Naomi Sheman, professor of philosophy and women's studies, University of Minnesota.

PARTNERSHIP BACKGROUND

In the 1980s, Susan Gust wanted to work on the issue of lead poisoning in her neighborhood, the economically disadvantaged Phillips section of south Minneapolis. She had been to a community organizing training and thought she needed to find an "enemy" to work against. Gust and other members of the Phillips Lead Collaborative first approached the University of Minnesota, which has a clinic in the neighborhood, as the enemy because of a past perception of the university as "only being in the neighborhood when they needed something." Powerful entities such as universities were seen as able to receive grant money to work in the neighborhood while the neighborhood itself continued to get poorer.

Instead of the reaction she expected, Gust found the director of the clinic interested in working *with* her. They started working on designing collaborative research to document the lead problems in Phillips. It took time for the community members to believe it was worth doing the research, but eventually they became involved as researchers themselves—they were trained, paid for their time, and given "ownership" over the resulting data. They also realized that if they had the University of Minnesota as an ally, others (e.g., developers) would have a harder time exploiting the neighborhood.

The research they did helped create a pro-family city policy on how to deal with housing units where high lead levels were found, and additional lead-free units of housing were created. This project influenced the creation of ClearCorps, a national AmeriCorps program focused on lead abatement.

HOW THE PARTNERSHIP WORKS

At the meetings of the collaborative, people need to answer only three questions to join:

(continued...)

1. What is your self-interest (both individual and organizational/institutional, if applicable)?

2. What do you have to contribute to the group?

3. What do you want to learn?

Decisions are made collaboratively; even issues like research structure (e.g., using control groups) are open for discussion. The group determines who gets listed as authors on reports and chooses university and community representatives to co-present project findings at conferences or to the legislature.

ADVICE FOR OTHERS

Mutual respect is essential. Community members should understand that higher education is relevant to their lives. Higher education creates knowledge that affects everyone, and can influence those in power. Campus members should recognize that community taxes support higher education, and that community members should have a say in research and other work that affects them.

Campus and community partners should have a written "covenant" for working together—not something as formal as a contract, but a memorandum of agreement that covers what the parties are doing together and what they want out of the relationship. It is also helpful to address at the outset how and when the partnership should end. Having the community representatives write the agreement can help ease a perceived power imbalance.

Training on dealing with power issues is critical. Specific measures that can smooth power issues include deciding not to use "Dr." or other titles, agreeing in advance on who will run meetings and write minutes, and teaching conflict resolution techniques. It is important for community and campus partners to strive to know each other as people and to understand each other's cultures so they can talk things through when difficult issues arise.

Ongoing monitoring and accountability are necessary to ensure that the partnership experience is working for the community organization's clients or others in the community. Celebration of each other's roles and accomplishments should also be ongoing. In particular, community people need to see themselves as teachers and to be respected in that role.

groups to build or rehabilitate facilities for shared use. If you are already working with someone on campus, ask about facilities use. If you do not currently have a relationship but would like to find out about use of facilities, call the Facilities office on campus for information or the Community Service Office to guide you to the appropriate office.

Some ways that community organizations might use campus facilities include:

- Use of classrooms, theaters, or dining halls for meetings, community forums, readings, or conferences.

- Use of theater, music, or gallery space for community plays, performances, or art exhibitions. These may be co-produced by campus and community partners, or just hosted by the campus.

- Use of athletic facilities by community residents or school groups.

- Use of green spaces for picnics, athletic events, protests, or community gatherings.

- Use of residence halls (typically during the summer) as affordable hotel, hostel, or retreat lodging.

- Use of libraries (including collections, books, magazines, music tapes, and computer terminals) by community residents.

- Use of empty office space, typically with affordable rent paid to the institution.

Institutions that are willing to share facilities range from small technical or community colleges to large universities. Following are examples of campuses with different types of facility sharing arrangements. These and other examples in this chapter are all from Minnesota, reflecting the experience of this volume's authors; campuses across the country offer similar arrangements.

Concordia University. Many meeting spaces are available on campus for use free of charge by off-campus groups. Some nonprofits have their offices on campus. The community is strongly encouraged to use the facilities. It is a presidential priority to share campus facilities freely with the public.

Metropolitan State University. The university worked in collaboration with the city of St. Paul to design and share the costs of building a new library on campus. The library serves both as the university library and as the public library in a neighborhood that previously had no local library.

Normandale Community College. The college and local cultural groups put together a joint cultural events calendar, including events at the college. In addition, the college offers free space for South Hennepin Adult Education ESL courses.

Southwest State University. Through the university's Center for Rural and Regional Studies, the campus sponsors a public History Center and provides the only public Geographic Information System (GIS) facility in the region.

Individual Expertise

Individual faculty and staff possess a wealth of expertise and talents that might be available to community organizations. In addition to serving as traditional volunteers, faculty, staff, and even alumni may work in the community in a variety of ways:

- **Advising.** Faculty or staff members with expertise in certain areas (for example, fundraising, demographic studies, environmental challenges, youth development) may be able to serve as informal or formal consultants for organizations.

- **Speaking.** Faculty or staff members can serve as keynote speakers, panelists, or trainers on a range of subjects.

- **Teaching.** Faculty may be willing to give groups of youth, scouts, senior citizens, or others a "mini-course" on their area of expertise.

- **Leading.** Faculty and staff can serve on boards of directors or advisory groups with nonprofit and government agencies.

- **Creating.** Arts and music faculty can be commissioned or invited to create public works of art or to perform at events.

Faculty Research

Faculty members, often with students, may complete research projects in community settings. For example, a class may administer a questionnaire about the health needs of immigrant women for a policy research action group; students may analyze data for a police department with the aim of improving police accountability in communities of color; or a faculty member may conduct research on rates of asthma in an inner-city neighborhood for a community heath organization to support recommendations for reducing automobile traffic.

There is a growing trend among faculty to conduct research collaboratively with community members. Such research might be co-designed with CBOs or other community members and executed by or with community members. Most important, the results may be used by community members in addressing community issues.

Research in the community can take several forms. Some projects are initiated by faculty members, while others may start with a community-identified need. Community-based research can result in real community improvement; projects may provide energy conservation technology in low-income housing, create new systems for providing more equitable police service within a municipality, or implement important programs to address community health. Categories of research follow.

If your organization has a particular project that would benefit from faculty involvement, contact the appropriate department or seek advice from the Community Service Office to find the expertise you need.

Community-based research. This is a general category that applies to all research in which the purpose is to understand issues affecting a particular community and in which community members, both individuals and organizations, are sources of information.

Collaborative research. Collaborative research refers to community-based research projects in which community members and faculty jointly set the research agenda, collect and analyze information, and share results.

Action research. Action research refers to a faculty-initiated project to study a community issue or organization, with the study planned to result in a particular action. The action might be a proposal to a government agency or a program evaluation. Although the researcher pursues the study out of a personal interest in the community or issue, the community members are generally not consulted and the results of the study are often not directly shared with the community.

Participatory action research. Participatory action research is pursued with the same goals as action research. In this form of research, however, one or more citizen's groups or CBOs identify the issue to be studied and seek assistance from a researcher or team of researchers. The results satisfy a community-identified agenda rather than a faculty-generated agenda.

Advocacy research. Advocacy research is a subcategory of participatory action research where the goal is to use the research results to persuade policymakers to take specific actions on behalf of citizen's groups and/or CBOs that are concerned about a particular community problem.

Empowerment research. Empowerment research is done on behalf of, and in conjunction with, underrepresented, resource-poor groups and organizations. The goal of the research is to increase the effectiveness of these groups in influencing policy decisions that affect them.

Academic Resources

Many institutions offer courses, seminars, conferences, continuing education classes, and other forms of training that are appropriate for—or even designed for—community members. Some institutions make academic resources more accessible by offering community members special rates on training programs, offering courses free of charge, or providing community scholarships to attend the college or university. Following are some examples of campuses that have specific policies in place to share academic resources.

Augsburg College. Augsburg has created a scholarship program for a local partnering K-8 school, where children receive $1,000 in scholarship money to Augsburg for each year they complete at the K-8 school.

Augsburg also offers a $5,000 scholarship for AmeriCorps members who choose to attend the college.

Bethel College. Bethel has developed scholarships for residents of the Frogtown–Summit University neighborhoods (where Bethel has several community partnerships) to earn an undergraduate degree in business, organizational leadership, or one of several other areas. Two full scholarships per cohort in each academic program are set aside for this purpose.

Concordia College. Every February, Concordia offers community residents a "Communiversity" program with a catalog of academic options in areas ranging from music to finance. These mini-courses are co-taught by faculty and community residents.

Minnesota State Colleges and Universities. The MNSCU campuses offer scholarships to first-generation college students (those who are first in their families to attend college). The scholarships cover the cost of students' first course, books, and supplies.

North Hennepin Community College. North Hennepin offers a "Women in Leadership" program as well as scholarships to attend. Half of the participants in the most recent program came from nonprofit and immigrant groups who received scholarships to participate and then brought what they learned back to their organizations. The development office at the college also works with the local Rotary Club to offer college scholarships to at-risk youth.

University of St. Thomas. As part of its business school, the university established a Center for Nonprofit Management that offers "mini-MBA" programs to local nonprofit leaders as well as free seminars to develop the capacity of the nonprofit community in St. Paul/Minneapolis area. St. Thomas also offers free computer training to senior citizens.

Community Development Initiatives

Institutions of higher education are major employers and purchasers of goods and services. Some institutions have special programs to improve the economic base and vitality of the neighborhoods where the campus is located. These might include:

- Partnerships with local job training programs;

- Contracts to purchase goods or services locally;

- Investment of endowment resources or other finances in community development financial institutions to encourage small business loans;

- Campus "greening" initiatives to reduce waste or use alternative energy sources;

- Real estate development programs to create or improve affordable housing;

- Voluntary financial contributions to community nonprofits or municipal services (police, fire, etc.), for which higher education is tax exempt.

Some examples of community development initiatives follow.

College of St. Scholastica. Vendors from the local area who submit bids for college contracts are allowed to match or counter bids that are made by non-local vendors.

Hamline University. Hamline contributed $15,000 and expertise to community efforts to redesign Snelling Avenue. The university also gives $12,000 every year to a key community partner, the Hamline-Midway Coalition, for its operating expenses.

Macalester College. Macalester College built a wind turbine on the campus to help offset energy costs.

Metropolitan State University. Management, security, and maintenance of facilities are contracted out to local companies; the university seeks minority- and women-owned businesses for these purposes.

St. Olaf College and Carleton College. St. Olaf is using a portion of its endowment to create a community development fund in partnership with Carleton College.

University of Minnesota, Twin Cities. The university has established an office charged with doing business with women and minority-owned businesses. The university also adheres to an agreement to refrain from buying foreign products made through exploitive labor practices.

Partnership Creation Resources

Elements of Effective Partnerships

1. HONESTY AND TRUST: A climate and culture of honesty and trust must be established.

2. BROAD STAKEHOLDER REPRESENTATION: Partnerships must include stakeholders from as many sectors of the community as possible. Anyone who may have an interest in the partnership or be affected by it should be invited to participate.

3. RECIPROCITY: The relationship should be symbiotic, benefiting all partners.

4. ROLES AND RESPONSIBILITIES—A DIVISION OF LABOR: Leadership, decision making, responsibility, and use of resources must be shared.

5. NEEDS/CHALLENGES/RESOURCES/ASSETS: Partnerships need to perform a needs/challenges/resources/assets assessment to help them establish the direction of the partnership and help it to form its mission.

6. VISION AND MISSION: Partnerships must establish a common vision and mission that is free to change or adjust as the partnership progresses.

7. GOALS, OBJECTIVES, AND AN ACTION PLAN: The partnership needs to collectively agree on its goals, develop objectives to address these goals, and create an action plan to meet the goals and objectives identified.

8. COMMUNICATION: Regular and effective communication must be planned and maintained.

9. ASSESSMENT: There needs to be a formative and summative assessment of process and outcomes.

10. CELEBRATION OF EFFORTS: The partnership must plan for and celebrate its efforts and recognize the partners for their hard work.

SOURCE: *K-H Partnerships Toolkit.* Concord, NH: Campus Compact for New Hampshire (www.compactnh.org/resources.htm). Reprinted by permission.

Expectations for Site Supervisors

This guide, from the Service-Learning Institute at the University of California-Monterey Bay, was developed for CBOs working with students who are on site as part of a class requirement (service-learning). Most of the information, however, applies equally to student volunteers whose work is not tied to a particular course.

A. READ THE COURSE SYLLABUS.

Communicating with the faculty person to learn about the course content will help you shape the student's learning experience and understand what the student is bringing to the placement. Keep in mind that not only do service-learning students want to help meet important community needs, but they are also using the experience as the basis for understanding their college course. Students are receiving academic credit for learning through their service efforts. Help students think about what the experience means to them, the organizational context, and overall societal issues and impacts.

B. PROVIDE A JOB DESCRIPTION.

A clear service-learning job description, outlining tasks, responsibilities, and required skills must be prepared and given to the student. Positions that carry some degree of responsibility and involve client contact are ideal.

C. BE SELECTIVE.

Be aware that some students may not match your needs. Although the Service Learning Institute will refer student service-learning candidates to your agency, you will make the final selection. If a student's qualifications and/or motivations are not in harmony with your needs, it is your right and obligation to request a different student.

D. ORIENT, TRAIN, AND SUPERVISE!

Students require a carefully structured orientation to your agency, staff, and clients. Introduce them to staff, provide a tour of the facility, discuss emergency policies, accident procedures, and the rules and regulations of the site. Explain your mission and familiarize students with key community and societal issues facing your organization (i.e., "the bigger picture"—why you do what you do, and how the student can contribute to this end). Use the "Orientation Checklist" provided in the next section to help you plan your orientation.

E. BE REALISTIC WITH YOUR TIME COMMITMENT AND EXPECTATIONS OF STUDENTS.

Think in terms of semesters and the academic calendar. Remember that you will have to be aware of the semester schedule and adapt accordingly (offer training sessions during the early part of the semester and expect students for an average of 3–5 hours a week for a 10-week period).

F. BE AN INVOLVED TEACHER AND MENTOR FOR STUDENTS.

The supervisor is truly a partner in the student's education and should view her/himself as an educator. Throughout the assignment help the student interpret the experience and the relationship between what he/she is doing and the work of the agency and others. At the beginning of the semester, the student will ask you to review and sign his or her Service Learning Plan. This plan will clarify the student's learning objectives and job responsibilities. Your relationship with the student is one of the most significant elements of the service-learning experience and often determines the success of the placement.

G. SAY "THANK YOU" TO STUDENTS.

Like everyone, students want to be welcome and appreciated. This may take many forms, from letters of recognition to a thank you note or a verbal acknowledgment of a job well done. They also need to see how their work is important to your agency's mission. Ask the students how they're doing and what could be improved.

H. TALK TO US—COMPLETE AND RETURN TWO EVALUATIONS.

Keep the Service Learning Institute staff informed of any concerns, suggestions, or other pertinent issues related to the placement and/or the student. We are here to facilitate the process and assist you in any way possible.

SOURCE: *Service Learning Guide for Community Partners,* Service Learning Institute, California State University-Monterey Bay (http://service.csumb.edu/partners/partner_guide.html). Reprinted by permission.

Orientation Checklist

The *Orientation Checklist* below is a tool to help you properly prepare service learners for their community experiences. The orientation should provide students with a clear understanding of the work they will be doing, any risk associated with that work, and how they should conduct themselves when they are working in the community as part of a class assignment.

The first orientation, prior to the first day of service, gives students information about the community-based organization and the nature of their service placements. This should take place on campus, either in class or in a required outside-of-class meeting.

The second orientation, presented by the community-based organization, should take place at the site where students will be working. This is the simplest, most effective way for students to become aware of emergency policies, accident procedures, and the rules and regulations of the site.

ORIENTATION PROVIDED BEFORE THE FIRST DAY OF SERVICE

1. Mission of the community-based organization (CBO).

2. Who does the CBO serve?

3. What programs/service does the CBO offer?

4. Specific policies and procedures related to the service placement.

5. Review any proof of eligibility that is needed (fingerprinting, background check). Who will cover the cost of this? Where should students go to have fingerprinting done?

6. Discuss CBO volunteer expectations.

7. Provide students a job description detailing the work they will do (outlining the scope of work). Explain the types of activities that are outside the scope of work.

8. Give the students their site supervisor's contact information.

9. Will the students need to meet with the site supervisor prior to beginning their service?

10. How closely will the student be supervised? By whom?

11. Who do the students call if they cannot make their scheduled service, or will be late?

12. Discuss appropriate attire when providing service (based on CBO standards).

13. Provide specific training for the position.

14. What will the student learn? What qualities or skills will the student develop?

15. Review confidentiality rules for the site. Are pictures or video allowed?

16. Review the risks associated with this placement.

17. Explain what students should do if harassment occurs. Who do they contact?

18. Talk about the service schedule (total number of hours, days and times of the week, etc.). Also discuss the beginning and end of service. Students should not volunteer outside of scheduled hours until the requirement is complete.

19. Who can the students contact with questions or concerns about their placement (CBO contact and campus contact)?

20. Is there a CBO training or orientation to attend? Where? When? How long?

21. Where do students check in at the site on their first day?

22. How are students' service hours recorded? (For their course and the CBO.)

23. Give the location of the site and directions via personal vehicle or public transportation. Where will students park if they drive? What is the cost associated with parking or taking public transit? Emphasize that the student is responsible for getting to and from the site.

24. Who will be evaluating the students' service? Is there a formal evaluation the CBO will fill out?

ON-SITE ORIENTATION (ON OR BEFORE THE FIRST DAY OF SERVICE)

1. Tour of site—location of restroom and break room.

2. Where, and with whom, do students check in each time they arrive at the site?

3. Where is the logbook kept (to record service hours)?

4. Review safety rules of the site, location of emergency exits, and emergency procedures.

5. Introduce students to other staff at the agency.

6. Emergency contact information: ask students' permission to share with university.

7. Review accident procedures at the site and what to do if a student or client is hurt.

SOURCE: *Service Learning Guide for Community Partners,* Service Learning Institute, California State University-Monterey Bay (http://service.csumb.edu/partners/partner_guide.html). Reprinted by permission.

Part III

Creating Long-Term Success

Building Sustainable Partnerships

Although all partnerships are different, community-campus partnerships that have endured and grown over time do share a number of characteristics. In general, these partnerships take many years to develop. Most began as a single project or program that evolved as relationships deepened and new opportunities for collaboration emerged. As they evolve, these partnerships often grow both in the range of activities they offer and in the number of partners involved.

This chapter examines different levels of partnerships, reviews characteristics of successful long-term partnerships, and offers case studies with examples of sustained partnerships. These examples are not necessarily meant to represent the "ideal" partnership; rather, they reflect the diversity of communities and institutions that are served by sustained partnerships.

Levels of Partnership

The depth of relationships between campuses and community organizations varies widely. Some partnerships exist to fill a specific need or opportunity, while others are much deeper and more complex. Although either type of relationship can be sustained, deeper partnerships are more likely to be long-lasting as well as to offer the potential for both the campus and the CBO to improve their practice.

That said, the level of involvement does not make the relationship good or bad. As long as there is respect on both sides for the strengths and knowledge that all partners bring to the relationship, the partnership is likely to remain strong. The levels of campus-community partnerships described below do not reflect every situation, nor do they necessarily represent a progression that will work best for any given partnership. They are presented simply to raise awareness of the possibilities. It should be noted that because of the complexity of higher education institutions and community organizations, relationships reflecting various degrees of partnership may exist in different parts of the same institution or organization.

LEVEL 1. LIMITED AWARENESS OF EACH OTHER

At this level, the relationship may involve infrequent contact by one individual or posting of an open position.

- The CBO may have a listing with the institution for volunteers or interns that students occasionally fill.

- Communication is limited to updating the listing now and then.

- No strong personal relationships exist between campus and community representatives.

- There is little or no expectation on either side of a continued relationship.

LEVEL 2. LIMITED ACTIVITIES AND EXPECTATIONS

At this level, the CBO and the college have a predictable but limited relationship that may involve one or a few people each term.

- The CBO may post a listing for volunteers, interns, or service-learning students once every term or academic year.

- One or a few people from the institution work with the community organization in predictable ways.

- The community partner has a contact on campus, but communication is limited to a few conversations or emails each year.

- There is an expectation on both sides that a few positions will be filled or that certain specific events will happen each year.

- Agreements and expectations may or may not be written down.

LEVEL 3. STRUCTURED INVOLVEMENT

At this level, involvement between the partners is consistent and may take multiple forms, and some structures have been put in place for staffing, communication, and other functions.

- One or more groups of individuals from the institution are involved with the CBO each semester or year.

- Examples may include a service-learning course or multiple courses whose students serve with the organization each semester; work-study students filling positions at the organization to coordinate other volunteers from campus; student, faculty, and community researchers regularly working together on community-based action research projects; a large group of students or staff completing valuable volunteer projects several times each year; or a combination of types of involvement.

- There are clear lines of communication between campus and community contact people, and communication is regular and open.

- Both sides have expectations for the types and quality of involvement.

- The relationship involves some joint planning, and the partners may complete some type of evaluation together.

- Some written documents exist to clarify expectations and plans.

- The campus and CBO may make facilities and other resources available for use by the partner.

LEVEL 4. JOINT PROJECT DEVELOPMENT

Organizations at this level of partnership work with their campus partners to design initiatives that address issues of common concern.

- In addition to potential forms of involvement described in Level 2, campus and community partners work together to address issues in ways that neither could accomplish on their own. Examples include creating new community programs (e.g., community health care, literacy programs, small business development) that are identified as the collaborative efforts of equal partners.

- Fundraising, evaluation, and marketing are done jointly.

- Resources, information, and publicity benefit both partners equally or nearly equally.

- Communication is clear and open.

- Power in determining the future of the collaborative is discussed openly and shared.

LEVEL 5. COLLABORATION BASED ON RISK AND RESOURCE SHARING
- In relationships that reach this stage, the partners understand that each one's success in the venture is bound to the other's.

- In addition to elements of Level 3 and Level 4, initiatives at this level are characterized by full collaboration in sharing risks and resources, including funding and staff. An example would be a joint organization or coalition created to address complex community issues requiring significant planning and coordination of resources.

- Governance of the new group does not favor any partner or interest.

- If a primary partner in the work changes, the entire collaboration changes.

- All partners are able to articulate their self-interests and assist the other members of the collaboration in reaping benefits from working together.

To a certain extent, these five degrees of involvement between community organizations and campuses can be viewed as steps to take in managing the progression of the partnership. They may also serve as signposts to evaluate where the partnership is and the degree to which the partners are satisfied with the status quo. For organizations that are in the early stages of a partnership, Level 1 and Level 2 are natural levels of involvement. As the partners become more comfortable working with each other, and as mutual benefits are achieved, they may naturally move towards Level 3 and Level 4. Partnerships that reach Level 5 are fairly rare. Because they require the trust and long-term commitment of all parties involved, they usually arise from an already long-standing relationship.

Characteristics of Long-Term Success

In *Benchmarks for Campus/Community Partnerships* (Campus Compact, 2000), Campus Compact identifies three main characteristics of partnerships that are sustained over time.

First, such partnerships are **integrated into the mission and support systems of the partnering institutions.** As *Benchmarks* notes:

> The most effective way to sustain a partnership over time is to secure the support of influential neighborhood institutions, and to spread the work of the partnership throughout your own institution. Successful partnerships are aligned with their institutional missions, [often] linked to the academic curriculum, and have full institutional support.... Ideally, a partnership both reflects and influences the priorities of the sponsoring institutions (pp. 26–27).

Second, partnerships are **sustained by a "partnering process" for communication, decision making, and the initiation of change.**

> A strong partnership process is one that responds to change even as it works to realize an ambitious, long-term goal. It provides ample opportunity for the sharing of opinions and ideas. This solidifies the commitment of partners to collaborate over time, and facilitates their ability to change direction and redefine their work as the world around them changes. Three major elements that form the basis of a strong partnership process are practices that support frequent communication with partners and with the immediate community; a method for revisiting the essential elements of the partnership and making decisions; [and] a structure that allows for evolution, change, and growth (p. 30).

Third, sustained partnerships are **evaluated regularly with a focus on both methods and outcomes.**

> When it works best, evaluation is integrated into daily operations and long-term objectives and becomes a tool to improve the partnership rather than simply a report on its successes and failures.... The process of assessment serves a valuable role in convening participants and asking them to reflect individually and as a group on their methods and goals. Assessment institutionalizes critical analysis. For this reason it is most useful when viewed as a continuous process that begins when the partnership does (p. 34).

Community-Campus Partnerships for Health, a national nonprofit organization that promotes health through partnerships between communities and higher education institutions, outlines the following characteristics of successful community-campus partnerships:[1]

1. Partners have agreed upon mission, goals, and measurable outcomes for the partnership.

2. The relationship between partners is characterized by mutual trust, respect, genuineness, and commitment.

3. The partnership builds upon identified strengths and assets, but also addresses issues that need improvement.

4. The partnership balances power among partners and enables resources among partners to be shared.

5. There is clear, open, and accessible communication between partners, making it an ongoing priority to listen to each need, develop a common language, and validate/clarify the meaning of terms.

6. Roles, norms, and processes for the partnership are established with the input and agreement of all partners.

7. There is feedback to, among, and from all stakeholders in the partnership, with the goal of continuously improving the partnership and its outcomes.

8. Partners share the credit for the partnership's accomplishments.

9. Partnerships take time to develop and evolve over time.

Drawing on these two sets of characteristics, some general observations can be made. First, successful community-campus partnerships are characterized by a **shared commitment** on the part of the partners to equality and reciprocity. In effective, sustained partnerships, the community and higher education partners are equal players, each of which brings important assets that are mutually recognized and valued by the partners.

---

1. Community-Campus Partnerships for Health, *Principles of Good Community-Campus Partnerships* (http://depts.washington.edu/ccph/principles.html#principles). Used by permission. Note: The website also offers articles on putting these principles into practice.

Second, **frequent communication** among the partners is crucial to the success of the partnership. Communication among the partners involves not only planning and coordination of partnership activities, but ongoing feedback as well.

Third, **ongoing evaluation** is an important element of the communication process. Evaluation should include not only assessment of continuing and completed projects but also of the partnership itself.

As your partnership grows it is important that you and your higher education partner(s) communicate about the degree to which the characteristics outlined above are present in your partnership and/or whether they are agreed upon goals to be achieved.

See page 85 for indicators of best practices in sustaining partnerships.

Creating Sustainable Structures

One of the challenges to sustaining community-campus partnerships is that they are often built on close personal relationships. These personal connections are necessary for building trust and reciprocity between the partners. Unfortunately, partnerships can be vulnerable if individuals move, or retire, or make career changes. One mechanism for sustaining community-campus partnerships in the event of personnel changes is to create a physical structure or center for partnerships. There are several ways to bring this about:

- Encourage the various faculty, departments, and offices on campus that regularly work with community organizations to coordinate and combine their efforts. Participate on an advisory committee to realize that effort. Likewise, invite college personnel to serve on your board of trustees.

- Encourage the campus administration to apply for a Community Outreach Partnership Center (COPC) grant from the U.S. Department of Housing and Urban Development. This federal grant program provides three-year seed grants for the purpose of institutionalizing campus-community partnerships.

- Explore joint funding opportunities. Most CBOs have had to develop fundraising expertise. Likewise, most colleges and universities have well-staffed development offices. Your mutual fundraising goals can be enhanced by sharing expertise and knowledge of funding sources and by developing collaborative grant proposals.

Examples of Sustained Community-Campus Partnerships

SOUTHSIDE INSTITUTIONS NEIGHBORHOOD ALLIANCE, HARTFORD, CT

The Southside Institutions Neighborhood Alliance (SINA)—a collaboration among Trinity College, Hartford Hospital, the Institute for Living, Connecticut Public Broadcasting, and Connecticut Children's Medical Center—has worked for more than 25 years to address pressing issues in their shared community.

Perhaps the most noteworthy result of this partnership has been the planning and construction of The Learning Corridor, an education-focused neighborhood revitalization project. SINA raised $120 million for the project over five years, including public and private support. The project focuses on a 15-block area near Trinity College in Hartford's South End, one of the state's poorest neighborhoods.

Construction on The Learning Corridor began in 1998, and by 2000 four new public schools had opened: an elementary school, and middle school, the Greater Hartford Academy of Math and Science, and the Greater Hartford Academy of the Arts. Staff members at the SINA partnering organizations offer professional expertise and guidance to students at the new schools. The Learning Corridor also includes a new Boys and Girls Club, located on the Trinity campus and staffed by Trinity students; a job training and career counseling center; a technology center that offers low-cost computer courses for community members; and a social services agency. In addition, the project tapped into funds from the U.S. Department of Housing and Urban Development to refurbish more than 20 neighborhood homes, which were then sold to local residents.

The Learning Corridor has received widespread praise for its success in revitalizing the neighborhood and adding to the quality of life of the city. A chief source of this success is the ability of the community and higher education partners to work together to serve the community. As a report from partner Connecticut Public Broadcasting notes, "However impressive the construction of new schools and an expansive new public space may be, it is the building of partnerships between the institutions and the community that is the true investment in the future."[2]

THE WEST PHILADELPHIA IMPROVEMENT CORPS, PHILADELPHIA, PA

The West Philadelphia Improvement Corps (WEPIC) began 20 years ago as the result of an honors history seminar at the University of Pennsylvania in which students studied youth unemployment in West Philadelphia. The students proposed the creation of a youth corps that would make use of existing agencies and resources. The university's Center for Community Partnerships describes the corps this way:[3]

> WEPIC is now a year-round program that involves approximately 10,000 children, their parents, and community members in educational and cultural programs, recreation, job training, community improvement, and service activities. WEPIC seeks to create comprehensive, higher education-assisted community schools that are the social, service delivery, and educational hubs for the entire community. Ultimately, WEPIC intends to help develop schools that are open 24 hours a day and function as the core building of the community.

> WEPIC is coordinated by the West Philadelphia Partnership—a mediating, nonprofit community-based organization composed of institutions (including Penn), neighborhood organizations, and community leaders—in conjunction with the School District of Philadelphia. Other WEPIC partners include community groups, communities of faith, unions, job training agencies, and city, state and federal agencies and departments.

> WEPIC supports evening and weekend, extended-day, and school-day programs. The evening and weekend programs offer a wide range of educational and cultural classes for children and adults as well as sports and crafts. Community councils provide guidance on program content. Classes are taught by public school teachers, community members, and Penn staff and students. Extended-day and school-day programs emphasize the integration of service-learning with academ-

---

2. Connecticut Public Broadcasting, *The Learning Corridor: A Hartford Success Story* (www.cpbi.org/pdf/LearningCorridor.pdf).

3. Center for Community Partnerships, University of Pennsylvania, *West Philadelphia Improvement Corps* (www.upenn.edu/ccp/wepic_hist.shtml).

ics and job-readiness. WEPIC has developed service-learning programs that are integrated across the curriculum and engage students
in creative work designed to advance skills and abilities through serving their schools, families, and community. Focus areas include health
and nutrition, the environment, conflict resolution/peer mediation,
reading improvement, desktop-published school/community newspa-
pers, technology, and construction training.

The academic work done with the WEPIC schools is based upon a
community-oriented, real world, problem-solving approach. Activities
are focused upon areas chosen by each school's principal and staff. In
this neo-Deweyan approach, students not only learn by doing, but also
learn by and for service. WEPIC schools serve, educate, and activate
students, their families, and other local residents. The idea behind this
approach is that schools can function as the strategic and catalytic
agents for community transformation.

POLICY RESEARCH ACTION GROUP, CHICAGO, IL

Founded in 1989, the Policy Research Action Group (PRAG) is a consor-
tium of community-based and community-focused nonprofit organizations and urban universities in the Chicago area focused on researching
health, social, and other issues that affect community life. According to
PRAG director Philip Nyden, PRAG "grew out of the need felt by pro-
gressive researchers and community-based leaders for a more systematic
connection between university and community resources in addressing
policy issues ranging from gentrification and displacement of poor families to the negative impact of toxic wastes and emissions on low-income
communities." [4]

To date, PRAG has supported more than 175 collaborative research projects between university researchers and community-based organizations.
The participating universities are Chicago State University, DePaul
University, Loyola University of Chicago, National-Louis University, and
the University of Illinois, Chicago. They work with a range of community organizations and members.

---

4. Nyden, Philip, "Partnerships for Collaborative Action Research." In Jacoby, Barbara
(Ed.). *Building Partnerships for Service-Learning*. San Francisco: Jossey-Bass, 2003, p. 213.

Among Nyden's recommendations from his experience with PRAG are two with particular relevance for CBOs:

- **Tailor collaborative research to the institution and the community.** There is no one-size-fits-all collaborative research model.... Creating a unique model that meets institutional and community needs is part of the enjoyment of collaborative research work.

- **Start small.** Large networks do not start overnight. Starting with limited collaborative projects, and gradually building larger networks or centers, is the route that most established centers have taken.... The beauty of this kind of work is that it can start with one faculty member or one class working in partnership with one community organization.

Assessing Partnerships

No matter what type of partnership you have, from a small-scale project to a broad collaboration, ongoing assessment is a key to success. Evaluation helps identify emerging issues before they become problems and provides a mechanism for continual quality improvement. It also fosters open communication among partners, which strengthens relationships and validates multiple points of view.

Two types of evaluation are relevant, each with distinct processes and goals. First is evaluation of the partnership itself and its activities. What is working well? What needs improvement? Are structures in place for addressing any issues that arise? Second is evaluation of how the partnership, successful or not, affects your organization. Do the benefits outweigh the costs? If not, what changes can be made to shift the equation?

Following are two assessment templates, one for each type of evaluation. Although they include specific information such as questions to be answered, benchmarks, issues, and solutions, this information is meant as a guideline. You will need to adapt any assessment tool to reflect your specific situation.

Evaluating Partnerships

The assessment rubric below is based on the partnership framework outlined in Campus Compact's *Benchmarks for Campus/Community Partnerships* (Campus Compact, 2000). That framework reflects three facets of partnerships: values, organization, and processes. These facets are present to varying degrees across the main stages of partnership development.

VALUES

BENCHMARK	STAGE 1: DESIGNING THE PARTNERSHIP	STAGE 2: BUILDING ON COLLABORATION	STAGE 3: SUSTAINING THE PARTNERSHIP
Shared vision and clearly articulated values	Partnering activities are based on individual projects rather than on a single partnership vision or mission statement.	The partners begin to explore longer-term projects and can identify the value of partnering as opposed to the benefits of isolated projects.	The partners have articulated a partnership vision or mission statement.
Mutual benefits to partners	Benefits are limited to achieving the short-term goals of a particular project or activity.	Partners are able to identify mutual benefits as opposed to benefits to each partner.	Partners build on each other's strengths in ways not envisioned before—e.g., joint membership on boards; joint grant writing, fundraising, and policy work.
Interpersonal relationships built on trust and mutual respect	Contact between community and campus partners is limited to a few phone calls, emails, and face-to-face meetings.	Contact between community and campus partners is more frequent. Partners become involved with the broader activities of the partnering organizations.	The partners have developed a collegial, professional relationship based on parity and mutual respect. They are comfortable with occasional disagreement and can offer constructive criticism.

ORGANIZATION

BENCHMARK	STAGE 1: DESIGNING THE PARTNERSHIP	STAGE 2: BUILDING ON COLLABORATION	STAGE 3: SUSTAINING THE PARTNERSHIP
Participation of multiple sectors	Participation is limited to a few individuals, primarily key campus staff, students, a few faculty, and the CBO director and/or volunteer coordinator.	One or a combination of partnering organizations coordinates activities among partners. Partners identify common community issues and problems.	Partnership activities among multiple organizations are coordinated in order to mobilize the relative strengths of each partner to meet common goals and objectives.
Clear organization and dynamic leadership	There is no partnership organization to speak of. The partnership encompasses ad hoc projects involving individual CBOs and various campus constituencies with no coordination.	The partnership organization takes the form of a task force or joint CBO-campus committee with regular meetings and shared communication among multiple partners.	The partnership itself has a permanent organization with a full-time director and staff.
Integration into the mission and support systems of the partnering institutions	Common values, such as service, are present in each partner's individual mission statement, but the partnership itself as a value is not recognized.	Partnership members articulate common mission and values and identify the values of the partnership per se.	The partnership as an institution has a clearly defined mission statement. Commitment to the partnership is also reflected in the mission and values statements of the partnering members.

PROCESSES

BENCHMARK	STAGE 1: DESIGNING THE PARTNERSHIP	STAGE 2: BUILDING ON COLLABORATION	STAGE 3: SUSTAINING THE PARTNERSHIP
"Partnership process" for communication, decision-making, and the initiation of change	Communication is infrequent and based on placement and project planning. There is little or no communication on mutual goals/benefits beyond particular projects.	Partners meet on a regular basis to discuss current and future projects. They set short-term and long-term partnership goals.	Partnership meetings are a regular part of joint planning, decision-making, and evaluation.
Regular evaluation with a focus on methods and outcomes	Evaluation is limited to community partners' evaluation of student participation and/or quality of the project.	Community partners' evaluation of projects and activities is incorporated into joint planning for service-learning and other community-based partnership activities.	In addition to regular evaluation of partnership activities, the partnership itself is regularly evaluated with input from all stakeholder groups.

Assessing Impact on Your Organization

In addition to assessing the partnership itself, you will want to consider the impact of the partnership on your organization. The benefits of partnership *potentially* outweigh the costs, but has that been the case for your organization? If not, what steps are necessary to realize those benefits? At what point do the actual costs outweigh the potential benefits, requiring that the partnership be restructured or even abandoned? This exercise will help you answer these questions.

STEP ONE: IDENTIFY THE COSTS OF THE PARTNERSHIP

Time

Calculate the amount of time staff spent training
and supervising student volunteers.

_____ hours/week

Calculate the amount of time staff spend
communicating with college/university personnel.

Face-to-face meetings	_____ hours/month
Phone conversations	_____ hours/week
Email	_____ hours/week

Calculate time lost that could be spent meeting with other constituencies
(e.g., board members, donors, public officials, etc.) that can be directly
attributed to time spent on partnership activities.

_____ hours/month

Financial Costs

Contribution to Federal Work Study student salaries, if applicable.

_____ month

Costs of new staff hired to support partnership activities, if applicable.

_____ month
(salary + benefits)

Costs of equipment used to support partnership activities.

_____ month

Intangibles

These are costs that cannot be calculated but that should be considered when you ask yourself whether the partnership is worth it.

Organizational Identity. Any outside influence, whether from funders, partners, or other sources, can affect your organization's identity and sense of mission. Ask yourself these questions to determine the impact of the partnership:

- To what degree has the partnership contributed to a loss of organizational identity and privacy?

- To what degree has the organization's core mission been diminished by the partnership?

Organizational Morale. Morale issues usually have to do with your staff's perception of their role in the partnership:

- Are the organization's staff treated with respect by students and campus staff and faculty?

- Is the staff's expertise and knowledge acknowledged and considered on par with the knowledge and expertise of the campus partner(s)?

- Do the staff enjoy working with students and faculty? Do they feel like co-educators when they work with students, or more like babysitters? Do they feel like colleagues when they work with campus faculty and staff or like underlings?

STEP TWO: CALCULATE THE BENEFITS OF THE PARTNERSHIP

Time

Calculate the staff time that is freed up by the partnership:

Staff time freed up by students/campus partners assuming organizational responsibilities.

_____ hours/week

Staff time freed up as a result of technical assistance/training from campus partners.

_____ hours/week

Calculate time spent with potential donors, public officials, etc. that can be directly attributed to the partnership.

_____ hours/month

Financial Benefits

Calculate the value added of student, faculty, and staff time contributed to the organization.

_____ hours/week
x $17.55/hour[1]

Calculate new revenue sources generated by the partnership, including grant dollars.

_____ month

---

1. Value of volunteer time calculated by Independent Sector, based on the average hourly earnings of nonagricultural workers as determined by the Bureau of Labor Statistics plus 12% to account for benefits (see www.independentsector.org/programs/research/volunteer_time.html).

Calculate the value of new equipment provided to the organization at no cost.

Total cost = _____

Calculate the value of facility space provided by the campus partner(s):

Square footage provided by campus partner(s) x average monthly lease cost per square foot in your area = _____.

Intangibles

Just as there are intangible costs, there are intangible benefits to partnerships.

Organizational Capacity. Your organization may have gained considerable capacity, both in manpower and in less tangible ways:

- In what ways has your organization's capacity to fulfill its core mission been enhanced by the partnership? Have new skills and resources been acquired as a direct result of the partnership? Has your organization gained additional recognition or prestige as a result of its connection to your campus partner(s)?

- Have you gained access to new donors? Has your ability to influence policymakers been enhanced?

- To what degree has research done by your campus partner(s) on your behalf increased your organization's effectiveness or aided in your advocacy work?

Organizational Morale. The same questions asked about organizational morale to identify intangible costs can also be asked to identify intangible benefits. Indeed, many community organizations cite the satisfaction of working with students and being treated as co-educators and knowledge experts in their own right as one of the key benefits of community-campus partnerships.

STEP THREE: COMPARE COSTS AND BENEFITS

Of course, the hope is that the numerical benefits of the partnership will outweigh the numerical costs. Even if they don't, you may find that the total benefits, including numerical and intangible benefits, outweigh the total costs, and that the benefits of the partnership meet or exceed your expectations. Conversely, you may find that the intangible costs outweigh the tangible benefits. If you are not seeing the expected benefits of the partnership, you and your campus partner(s) should have a serious discussion about what's not working and whether and how you can revitalize the partnership.

STEP FOUR: IDENTIFY PROBLEMS AND DEVELOP SOLUTIONS

On the following page is a trouble-shooting guide to help you think through problem areas in the partnership and how to fix them. Obviously, this chart doesn't cover every potential problem, but many of the common problem areas as reported by community and campus partners are listed here.

The problems noted here have a common characteristic. They are all examples of a lack of reciprocity and parity between community and campus partners. Likewise, they share a common solution—greater communication and coordination between partners. When reciprocity and open communication are present, the partnership is much more likely to live up to its potential.

PROBLEM	SOLUTION
Students are unreliable and/or disruptive.	Talk with the student first. Does unreliability stem from transportation problems or scheduling conflicts? Notify the campus volunteer coordinator or faculty member who arranged the student's placement. If the student has a transportation or scheduling problem, the campus partner can help identify solutions. If the student is disruptive, the campus partner can take appropriate disciplinary action.
The campus partner's priorities consistently take precedence over your priorities.	Communicate your concerns with your partner. Develop a set of shared priorities. If the problem persists despite your best efforts to correct it, consider terminating the partnership.
Your organization contributed information used in a campus research project, but the results of the research were never shared with the organization.	If a campus researcher approaches you about participating in a research project, find out ahead of time how the research will be used and how it will benefit the mission of your organization. If you perceive no benefit to your organization and the community you serve, don't participate. If the results are not shared with you, contact the appropriate oversight office on campus.[2]
Campus partner(s) receive funding for community-based research and/or community development, but do not share those funds or apply them directly to the community.	Identify the source of funds and the grant requirements. Meet with the grant manager and identify possible areas for resource sharing consistent with the program requirements. Discuss opportunities for a joint, externally funded project.
Faculty members send students to your site without coordinating with you to take into account your schedule and needs.	Just say no! Politely inform the faculty member in question that it is your policy to consult with faculty members and campus staff before students come to your organization. Let her/him know that the students will have a better experience and your clients will be better served if students have a basic understanding of your organization and the community you serve before they come to your site.

2. Most campuses have a coordinating office that ensures that all research conforms to legal and ethical requirements. If you believe that a faculty member has not met his/her obligations, report your concerns to that office.

Partnership Strengthening Resources

Building Lasting Partnerships: Best Practices

Below are three sets of indicators of best practices of successful community-campus partnerships. As you review these indicators, ask yourself the degree to which these characteristics are present in your partnership. Better yet, review them with your campus partner(s) to help identify the relative strengths and weaknesses of your partnership. Discuss areas for improvement and specify concrete actions that you can take together to meet those goals.

FROM **BENCHMARKS FOR CAMPUS/COMMUNITY PARTNERSHIPS**[1]
Successful partnerships that are democratic, collaborative, and sustainable over time are:

- Founded on a shared vision and clearly articulated values.

- Beneficial to all partnering institutions.

- Composed of interpersonal relationships based on trust and mutual respect.

- Multi-dimensional, involving participation of multiple sectors that act to address a complex problem.

- Clearly organized, with dynamic leadership.

- Integrated into the mission and support systems of the partnering institutions.

- Sustained by a "partnership process" for communication, decision-making, and the initiation of change.

- Evaluated regularly with a focus on both methods and outcomes.

---

1. Summarized from Torres, Jan (Ed.), *Benchmarks for Campus/Community Partnerships.* Providence, RI: Campus Compact, 2000.

FROM HIGHER EDUCATION-COMMUNITY PARTNERSHIPS: ASSESSING PROGRESS IN THE FIELD[2]

A measurement tool to determine whether partnerships were heading in the right direction included these elements:

- Community residents are integral in shaping the direction of collaborative projects.

- University administrators are supportive of campus-community partnerships.

- There is a shared commitment to capacity-building.

- Faculty are sensitive to community needs.

- There is a shared belief that partnerships will be mutually beneficial.

- The university's capacity is sufficient for the tasks.

- Community partners know how to take maximum advantage of university resources.

- Personal involvement exceeds a handful of committed community and university personnel.

- Third parties are brought in when necessary to act as brokers and intermediaries.

- Community participation includes the most disadvantaged community residents.

- Campus-community projects are related to broader collaborative efforts.

- There is joint exploration of separate and common goals and interests.

- The partners create a mutually rewarding, shared agenda.

2. Adapted from Maurrasse, David J., "Higher Education-Community Partnerships: Assessing Progress in the Field." *Nonprofit and Voluntary Sector Quarterly 31*(1) 2002: 131–139.

- The partners articulate clear expectations, capacities, and consequences for each partner.

- Success is measured in both institutional and community terms.

- Each partner shares control of partnership directions and/or resources.

- The partners focus on each other's strengths and assets.

- Partners identify opportunities for early success and regular celebration.

- Partners pay attention to communication and the open cultivation of trust.

- Partners are committed to continuous assessment of the partnership itself, as well as outcomes.

FROM BUILDING PARTNERSHIPS WITH COLLEGE CAMPUSES: COMMUNITY PERSPECTIVES[3]

The Council of Independent Colleges offers these core elements of effective partnerships that are worth sustaining:

- A set of mutually determined goals and processes, including processes to select and train people who will come into contact with a community organization or community residents.

- Shared vision, resources, rewards, and risks.

- A shared vision that is built on genuine excitement and passion for the issues at hand.

- Strategies focused on issues as they play out in a particular location, based on deep understanding of a community's interests, assets, needs, and opportunities.

---

3. Adapted from Liederman, Sally, Andrew Furco, Jennifer Zapf, and Megan Goss, Building Partnerships with College Campuses: Community Perspectives. Washington, DC: Council of Independent Colleges, 2003 (available for download at www.cic.edu/publications/books_reports/index.asp).

- A variety of roles and responsibilities based on each partner's particular capacities and resources.

- Peer relationships among faculty (and other campus partners) and management and staff of partner organizations in the community.

- Benefits (short or long-term) to each partner sufficient to justify the costs, level of effort, and potential risks of participation.

- A system of accountability that covers responsibility for carrying out jointly determined plans, ensuring that quality work is produced and benefits accrue to communities and campuses.

Appendices

Appendix 1:
Resources for Further Information

CAMPUS COMPACT

www.compact.org

As the only national organization dedicated solely to advancing higher education's civic mission, Campus Compact has been a leader in the movement to build civic learning into campus and academic life, with an emphasis on building communities. Partnership information and resources are available at www.compact.org/ccpartnerships.

NATIONAL SERVICE-LEARNING CLEARINGHOUSE

www.servicelearning.org

The National Service-Learning Clearinghouse (NSLC), a program of Learn and Serve America, operates a large service-learning website with timely information, thousands of free online resources, the nation's largest library of service-learning materials, national service-learning list-servs, and reference and technical assistance services.

LEARN AND SERVE AMERICA

www.learnandserve.org

Learn and Serve America supports service-learning programs in schools and community organizations that help nearly 1 million students from kindergarten through college meet community needs while improving their academic skills and learning the habits of good citizenship. Learn and Serve grants are used to create new programs or replicate existing programs, as well as to provide training and development to staff, faculty, and volunteers.

U.S. DEPARTMENT OF HOUSING AND URBAN DEVELOPMENT (HUD) OFFICE OF UNIVERSITY PARTNERSHIPS (OUP)

www.oup.org

HUD established the Office of University Partnerships (OUP) in 1994 to provide funding opportunities to encourage and expand the efforts of higher education institutions that are striving to make a difference in their communities. OUP's work helps increase the scope, effectiveness, and sustainability of higher education's community-building efforts.

HUD COMMUNITY OUTREACH PARTNERSHIP CENTERS (COPC)

www.oup.org/about/copc.html

The Community Outreach Partnership Centers (COPC) Program, an initiative of HUD's Office of University Partnerships, provides 3-year grants of up to $400,000 to encourage institutions of higher education to join in partnerships with their communities.

COMMUNITY-CAMPUS PARTNERSHIPS FOR HEALTH (CCPH)

http://depts.washington.edu/ccph

Community-Campus Partnerships for Health (CCPH) is a nonprofit organization that promotes health through partnerships between communities and higher educational institutions. CCPH has developed a range of partnership resources, available at http://depts.washington.edu/ccph/partnerships.html#Tools.

AMERICA'S PROMISE: THE ALLIANCE FOR YOUTH

www.americaspromise.org

The mission of America's Promise is to mobilize people from every sector of American life to build the character and competence of our nation's youth by fulfilling five promises: ongoing relationships with caring adults, safe places with structured activities, a healthy start, marketable skills, and opportunities to give back. Resources on the website include "Connecting Communities with Colleges & Universities."

THE ASSOCIATION FOR COMMUNITY AND HIGHER EDUCATION PARTNERSHIPS (ACHEP)

www.achep.com
ACHEP is a national membership organization that promotes, enhances, and sustains community-higher education partnerships aimed at improving the quality of life and opportunities available to residents of economically distressed communities.

CEOs FOR CITIES

www.ceosforcities.org
CEOs for Cities is a national bipartisan alliance of mayors, corporate executives, university presidents, and nonprofit leaders created to advance the economic competitiveness of cities.

HIGHER EDUCATION CONSORTIUM FOR URBAN AFFAIRS (HECUA)

www.hecua.org
HECUA provides students, faculty, and practitioners with necessary resources to help promote social transformation and community building.

NEW ENGLAND RESOURCE CENTER FOR HIGHER EDUCATION (NERCHE)

www.nerche.org
NERCHE is dedicated to improving colleges and universities as workplaces, communities, and organizations.

Appendix 2:
Wingspread Participants

The following education, community organization, and other leaders attended a conference on Community-Campus Partnerships held at the Wingspread Conference Center in Racine, Wisconsin, in April 2003, organized by Campus Compact with support from the Ford Foundation. This book resulted directly from the insight and information provided by these participants.

DON BADEN, Director, East St. Louis Project, Southern Illinois University-Edwardsville

JOHN BASSETT, President, Clark University

MARY BOMBARDIER, Community Partnership for Social Change, Hampshire College

DORIS BRIDGEMAN, Director of Youth Programs Community Investments, United Way of the Capital Area (Jackson, MS)

ROBERTA BUCHANAN, Executive Director, Howard Area Community Center (Chicago)

ARMAND W. CARRIERE, Office of University Partnerships, United States Department of Housing and Urban Development (HUD)

RICHARD CONE, University of Southern California

SUE DE VRIES, President, Garfield Development Corporation (Grand Rapids, MI)

JACQUELINE ELLIOT, Executive Director, Community Charter Middle School (San Fernando, CA)

SHIRLEY GIBSON, Council Member, North Dade Community Council 3 (Miami, FL)

MICHELLE D. GILLIARD, Council of Independent Colleges

GWENDA GREENE, Director of Service Learning, Gressette Leadership Center, Benedict College

DONALD HARWARD, Senior Fellow, Association of American Colleges and Universities (AAC&U)

BARBARA HOLLAND, Director, National Service-Learning Clearinghouse

WILLIAM HOWARD, Executive Director, West Humboldt Park Family and Community Development Council, DePaul University

BARBARA JACOBY, Director, Commuter Affairs and Community Service, University of Maryland-College Park

STEVEN JONES, Project Associate, Campus Compact

LARRY LITECKY, President, Century College

EDGAR LUCAS, JR., Executive Director, Renacer Westside Community Network (Chicago)

IRENE MARTINEZ, Coordinator, Active Learning Project, The Salvation Army-Phoenix

DAVID J. MAURRASSE, Founding Director, Center for Innovation in Social Responsibility, Columbia University

RICHARD MEISTER, Executive Vice President for Academic Affairs, DePaul University

REGINALD MILTON, Executive Director, South Memphis Alliance (Memphis, TN)

PHILIP NYDEN, Director, Center for Urban Research and Learning, Loyola University

MELISSA PEARCE, Memphis, TN

STEPHEN L. PERCY, Deputy Chancellor, The Milwaukee Idea, University of Wisconsin-Milwaukee

RICHARD PETERSON, Department of Information Decision Sciences, Montclair State University

WILLIAM M. PLATER, Executive Vice Chancellor and Dean of the Faculties, Indiana University-Purdue University Indianapolis

PAUL PRIBBENOW, President, Rockford College

JOHN SALTMARSH, Project Director, Campus Compact

JIM SCHEIBEL, Executive Director, Project for Pride in Living (Minneapolis)

SARENA D. SEIFER, Executive Director, Community-Campus Partnerships for Health, University of Washington

EVE ANN SHWARTZ, Executive Director, Partnership for Community Development (Hamilton, NY)

DIANE SONNEMAN, Co-Director, Griffin Center (East St. Louis, IL)

K. SUJATA, Executive Director, Apna Ghar (Chicago)

MARY LAUREL TRUE, Coordinator, Community Service Learning, Augsburg College

JILL WARREN, Executive Director, Indiana Campus Compact

MARSHALL WELCH, Director, Bennion Community Service Center, University of Utah

ANGELA WOODARD, Assistant Director of Service Learning, Gressette Leadership Center, Benedict College

LAURIE WORRALL, Executive Director, Stearns Center for Community Based Service Learning, DePaul University

Appendix 3:
Glossary of
Higher Education Terminology

Understanding the basic language of higher education, as well as complex issues such as tenure and faculty promotion, can give you insight into the culture of your higher education partner, leading to greater understanding of motivations and better chances for a productive and respectful relationship.

It is equally important that individuals from colleges and universities understand the language of your organization and the issues important to your community. Work with your higher education partner to teach each other important terminology as part of understanding each other's working environment and culture.

See pp. 25–27 for a discussion of different types of colleges and universities and what they can offer potential partners.

Following is a short list of some of the terms and concepts you are likely to come across in working with higher education institutions.

TYPES OF FACULTY

Higher education can be extremely hierarchical. Different labels (e.g., "instructor," "assistant professor") refer to different types of faculty positions that are generally associated with differing levels of stability and respect within academic institutions.

Faculty member. This is a general term used to describe all professors, instructors, and teachers at an institution. In some cases, only tenure-track professors (see "tenure," below) are formal members of the standing faculty.

Instructor. This term is generally used for faculty members at community and technical colleges, but may refer to a temporary or entry-level faculty member at other types of institutions.

Researcher. This position involves research but no classroom instruction.

Teacher's Aide (T.A.). This term usually refers to graduate students who assist faculty members by teaching all or some of a course and/or grading students' work.

Adjunct. An adjunct professor is a temporary or part-time faculty member.

Assistant/Associate Professor. Full-time professors who are on the tenure track (with the potential to become permanent faculty) start off as assistant professors. Once an assistant professor earns tenure, he or she is usually promoted to associate professor. Associate professors can be promoted to full professors. Assistant professors are also called junior faculty members, while associate and full professors are senior professors.

OTHER CAMPUS PERSONNEL

Alumni. A Latin word for graduates of an institution, referring to males or to males and females together. Other forms of the word include *alumnus* (singular male), *alumna* (singular female), and *alumnae* (plural female, most often used at women's colleges). Alumni may provide an invaluable connection between the campus and the community.

Community Service/Service-Learning Director. Many campuses now have a full- or part-time staff person in charge of community service and/or service-learning activities. These staff members are charged with making community connections and can offer valuable insight and assistance in navigating campus structures and procedures.

Dean/Provost/Vice-President for Academic Affairs. All of these terms can refer to the same person—the "chief academic officer" of an institution. This is the individual who is in charge of the faculty and oversees all things related to academic learning and research. A larger institution may have one provost or vice president who oversees the work of a number of deans (such as a dean for undergraduate studies and a dean of the law school). There are also deans and vice presidents for student affairs, who typically oversee student development, residential life, and other non-classroom aspects of student life. Any of these administrators may be a useful contact point for initiating a partnership.

President/Chancellor. This refers to the head of the institution overall. *President* is more common, used at colleges and most universities. *Chancellor* is typically used in a system with a primary state university that has a number of branch campuses; branch campuses typically have a chancellor, while the entire system may have a president.

Trustees/Regents. These terms usually refer to the individuals who serve on an institution's board of directors. Many are alumni of the institution or community leaders (or both). A trustee may serve not only on the board of the college but also on one or more CBO boards, providing a powerful ally for partnership work.

OTHER COMMONLY USED TERMS

Academic. This term can be a noun that refers to a person, such as a faculty member, or an adjective that refers to anything related to learning or research.

Assessment. Assessment in higher education usually refers to the ways that faculty members determine how well students are learning the academic subject matter of a course. Students are graded on what they learn and how well they show their learning through written assignments and tests. When faculty include a community-based learning experience in a course, they should be assessing what students learn from the experience, not how many hours they've logged.

Community college. Sometimes called junior colleges, these two-year institutions primarily serve students from the community, rather than from out of town. Community college students typically pay less than those at four-year institutions and earn a two-year associate's degree rather than a bachelor's degree. Many community colleges have an institutional commitment to their communities.

Department/Discipline/Division. Institutions of higher education are divided into departments, usually based on certain academic disciplines, or fields. *Department* refers to the actual grouping of faculty members and courses, usually in the same physical location, while *discipline* refers to the area of study. A *division* is an organizing concept used by some institutions to cluster certain departments and disciplines together, such as social sciences (which might include sociology, political science, anthropology, and economics) or humanities (which might include history and literature). Although in most institutions, partnership activity that involves faculty is arranged through individual faculty members, at some institutions whole departments may have a community mandate.

Distance learning. Distance learning or education refers to the growing phenomenon of institutions offering online courses over Internet, usually away from the campus location. Faculty may post assignments and discussion questions to a website for students read and reply to. Some institutions integrate service-learning with distance learning by asking students to complete a community experience in their home town, while the institution offering the online course may be hundreds of miles away.

Non-traditional student. The "traditional" college student graduates from high school and goes straight to college at age 18. Many of today's college students are older because they have taken time off between high school and college, are re-entering college after not finishing earlier, or are returning to school for a new degree or career. This population is growing; according to the Association for Non-Traditional Students in Higher Education, 47% of college students are now over the age of 25. These students may have less time but more life experience to offer CBOs.

Reflection. Reflection is the process of deriving meaning from experience. In many service-learning courses, faculty use reflection to help students make connections between their community experience and the academic subject matter of the course. They may ask reflective questions in class discussions or ask students to write reflective essays or journals, answering questions such as "What insights has your experience tutoring children given you regarding what is needed to prepare urban teachers?"

Semester/Quarter/Trimester/Term. All of these terms refer to ways that institutions define their calendar or year. The academic year is the part of the year where most classes take place, usually September–May, although this may vary, particularly as more institutions offer courses during the summer. A *semester* is the most common way to divide the academic year, usually with the fall semester running from September through December and the spring semester running from January through May. *Trimesters* break the year into three periods, usually a fall, spring, and summer period. *Quarters* can refer to half of a semester or to discrete fall, winter, spring, and summer periods. A *term* can refer to any of these periods.

Tenure. The tenure process is a years-long evaluation that can result in a faculty member gaining a permanent position, virtually guaranteeing his or her job through retirement. Only certain faculty positions (those on the tenure track) are eligible for this type of promotion. Tenured professors can be removed for inappropriate behavior, through consolidation of departments, or by a vote of the faculty, but otherwise they are unlikely to lose their jobs. Because the tenure process is so competitive, it can be difficult for faculty members to find time for community work unless such work is specified in the institution's tenure guidelines, which is rare.

University. Like four-year colleges, universities offer bachelor's degrees; the difference is that they include graduate schools that award advanced degrees in various disciplines, as well as professional schools such as law or medical schools. Because of their size, universities may have more—or at least more varied—resources available, but they may also be harder to navigate.

Bibliography

Books and Chapters

Bonnen, J.T. (1998). The land-grant idea and the evolving outreach university. In R.M. Lerner & Simon, L.A.K. (Eds.), *University-community collaborations for the twenty-first Century: Outreach scholarship for youth and families.* New York: Garland.

Cotton, D. & Stanton, T. (1990). Joining campus and community through service-learning. In C. Delve, S. Mintz, & G. Stewart (Eds.), *Community service as values education* (pp. 101–110). San Francisco: Jossey-Bass.

Hill, J. (Ed.) (1991). *You haven't to deserve: A gift to the homeless.* Atlanta, GA: Task Force for the Homeless.

Jacoby, B. (Ed.). (2003). *Building partnerships for service-learning.* San Francisco: Jossey-Bass.

Kemmis, D. (1945). *Community and the politics of place.* Norman, OK: University of Oklahoma Press.

Kretzman, J.P. & McKnight, J.L. (1993). *Building communities from the inside out: A path toward finding and mobilizing a community's assets.* Chicago: Urban Affairs and Policy Research Neighborhood Innovations Network, Northwestern University.

Lawson, H.A., & Hooper-Briar, K. (1994). *Expanding partnerships: Involving colleges and universities in interprofessional collaboration and service integration.* Oxford, OH: The Danforth Foundation and the Institute for Educational Renewal, Miami University.

Lerner, R.M., & Simon, L.A.K. (Eds.). (1998). *University-community collaborations for the twenty-first century: Outreach scholarship for youth and families.* New York: Garland Publishing.

Maurrasse, D. (2001). *Beyond the campus: How colleges and universities form partnerships with their communities.* New York: Routledge.

McKnight, J. (1995). *The careless society: Community and its counterfeits.* New York: Basic Books.

Minnesota Campus Compact. (1999a). *From charity to change: Model campus-community collaborations from Minnesota and the nation.* St. Paul, MN: Minnesota Campus Compact.

Minnesota Campus Compact. (1999b). *From charity to change: A notebook of resources from model campus-community collaborations from Minnesota.* St. Paul, MN: Minnesota Campus Compact.

Rhoads, R. (1997). *Community service and higher learning: Explorations of the caring self.* Albany, NY: State University of New York Press.

Shorr, L.B. (1989). *Within our reach: Breaking the cycle of disadvantage.* New York: Doubleday.

Shorr, L. (1997). *Common purpose: Strengthening families and neighborhoods to rebuild America.* New York: Anchor Books.

Sigmon, R. (1998). *Building sustainable partnerships: Linking communities and educational institutions.* Springfield, VA: National Society for Experiential Education.

Stack, C. (1974). *All our kin: Strategies for survival in a black community.* New York: Harper and Row.

Torres, J. (Ed.). (2000). *Benchmarks for campus/community partnerships.* Providence, RI: Campus Compact.

Vidal, A., et al. (2002). *Lessons from the community outreach partnership center program.* Washington, DC: U.S. Department of Housing and Urban Development Office of Policy Development and Research. Available at ww.oup.org/researchandpubs/copc/lessonslearned.html.

Walker, S. (Ed.) (1993). *Changing community.* St. Paul, MN: Greywolf Press.

Winer, M., & Karen, R. (1994). *Collaboration handbook: Creating, sustaining, and enjoying the journey.* St. Paul, MN: Amherst H. Wilder Foundation.

Zimpher, N.L., Percy, S.L., & Brukardt, M.J. (2002). *A time for boldness: A story of institutional change.* Bolton, MA: Anker Publishing.

Zlotkowski, E., Duffy, D.K., Franco, R. et al. (2004). *The Community's College: Indicators of Engagement at Two-Year Institutions.* Providence, RI: Campus Compact.

Articles and Reports

Adams, H. (1995). A grassroots think tank: Linking writing and community building. *Democracy and Education,* Winter.

America's Promise. (2004). *Connecting Communities with Colleges & Universities: Strategies to Strengthen Local Promise Efforts Through Higher Education Involvement.* Alexandria, VA: America's Promise. Available at www.americaspromise.org/products/litvid.cfm.

Arches, J., Darlington-Hope, M., Gerson, J., et al. (1997). New voices in university–community transformation. *Change, 29* (1), 36–44.

Boyle-Baise, M., Epler, B., & McCoy, W. (2001). Shared control: community voices in multicultural service-learning. *The Education Forum, 65* (4), 344–53.

Cone, D., & Payne, P. (2002). When campus and community collide: Campus-community partnerships from a community perspective. *The Journal of Public Affairs, 6,* 203–218.

Cruz, N., & Giles, D. (2000). Where's the community in service-learning research? *Michigan Journal of Community Service Learning,* Fall, 28–34.

Dorado, S., & Giles, D. (2004). Service-learning partnerships: Paths of engagement. *Michigan Journal of Community Service Learning,* Fall, 25–37.

Ducharme, E., Sargent, B. & Chaucer, H. (n.d.) The necessary elements. In N. Carriulo (Ed.), *Beginning and sustaining school college partner-*

ships. Winchester, MA: New England Association of Schools and Colleges.

Edwards, B., Mooney, L. & Heald, C. (2001). Whom is being served? The impact of student volunteering on local community organizations. *Nonprofit and Voluntary Sector Quarterly, 30* (3), 444–61.

Ferrari, J.R. & Worrall, L. (2000). Assessments by community agencies: How the "other side" sees service-learning. *Michigan Journal of Community Service Learning, 7,* 35–40.

Forrant, R. (2001). Pulling together in Lowell: the university and the regional development process. *European Planning Studies, 9* (5), 613–628.

Gamson, Z., Holland, E. & Kiang, P. (1998). The university in engagement with society. *Liberal Education,* Spring.

Gelmon, S., Holland, B., Seifer, S., Shinnamon, A & Connors, K. (1998). Community-university partnerships for mutual learning. *Michigan Journal of Community Service Learning, 5,* 97–107.

Goodrow, B. & Meyers, P.L. (2001). The Del Rio project: A case for community-campus partnership. *Education for Health: Change in Learning and Practice, 13* (2), 213–20.

Harkavy, I. & Puckett, J. (1991). Toward effective university-public school partnerships: An analysis of a contemporary model. *Teachers College Record, 92,* 556–581.

Holland, B. (2001). A comprehensive model for assessing service-learning and community-university partnerships. *New Directions for Higher Education, 114,* 51–60.

Kretzman, J. (1993). *School participation in local community economic development: Ideas for getting started.* Evanston, IL: Institute for Policy Research, Asset-Based Community Development, Northwestern University. Available at www.northwestern.edu/ipr/abcd.html.

Kreutziger, S.S., et al. (1999). The campus affiliates program. *American Behavioral Scientist, 42* (5), 827–39.

Liederman, S., Furco, A., Zapf, J. & Goss, M. (2003). *Building partnerships with college campuses: Community perspectives.* Washington, DC: The Council of Independent Colleges. Available at www.cic.org/publications/books_reports/index.asp.

Mayfield, L., Hellwig, M. & Banks, B. (1999). The Chicago response to urban problems: Building university-community collaborations. *American Behavioral Scientist, 42* (5), 863–875.

McHugh-Engstrom, C. and Tinto, V. (1997). Working together for service-learning. *About Campus,* July-August.

Morton, K. (1997). Campus and community at Providence College. *Expanding Boundaries,* Spring, 8–11.

Peacock, J.R., Bradley, D.B., & Shenk, D. (2001). Incorporating field sites into service-learning as collaborative partners. *Educational Gerontology, 27* (1), 23–36.

Pearson, N. (2002). Moving from placement to community partner. *The Journal of Public Affairs, 6,* 183–202.

Reardon, K.M. & Shields, T.P. (1997). Promoting sustainable community/university partnerships through participatory action research. *NSEE Quarterly, 23* (1), 22–25.

Saltmarsh, J. (1998). Exploring the meaning of community/university partnerships. *NSEE Quarterly, 23*(4).

Sandmann, L.R. & Baker-Clark, C.A. (n.d.) *Characteristics and principles of university-community partnerships: A delphi study.* Available at www.anrecs.msu.edu/ research/sandmann.htm.

Seifer, S. (1998). Service-learning: Community-campus partnerships for health professions education. *Academic Medicine, 73* (3), 273–277.

Speer, P.W. & Hughey, J. (1996). Mechanisms of empowerment: Psychological processes for members of power-based community organizations. *Journal of Community and Applied Social Psychology, 6,* 177–187.

Walsh, M.E., et al. (2000). The Boston College-Allston/Brighton partnership: Description and challenges. *The Peabody Journal of Education, 75* (3), 6–32.

Ward, K. & Wolf-Wendel, L. (2000). Community-centered service-learning: Moving from doing for to doing with. *American Behavioral Scientist, 43* (5), 767–80.

Weinberg, A.S. (1999). The university and the hamlets: Revitalizing low-income communities through university outreach and community visioning exercises. *American Behavioral Scientist,* 42 (5), 800–13.

W.W. Kellog Foundation. (n.d.) *Community partnerships toolkit.* Available at www.wkkf.org/Pubs/CustomPubs/CPtoolkit/CPToolkit/default.htm.

Zimmerman, M.A., & Rappaport, J. (1988). Citizen participation, perceived control, and psychological empowerment. *American Journal of Community Psychology, 16,* 725–750.